Research on Language and Social Interaction

VOLUME 32, NUMBER 3 — 1999

Table of Contents

Most Commonly Used Transcription Symbols

.	(period) Falling intonation.
?	(question mark) Rising intonation.
,	(comma) Continuing intonation.
-	(hyphen) Marks an abrupt cut-off.
::	(colon(s)) Prolonging of sound.
<u>never</u>	(underlining) Stressed syllable or word.
WORD	(all caps) Loud speech.
°word°	(degree symbols) Quiet speech.
>word<	(more than & less than) Quicker speech.
<word>	(less than & more than) Slowed speech.
hh	(series of h's) Aspiration or laughter.
.hh	(h's preceded by dot) Inhalation.
[ ]	(brackets) Simultaneous or overlapping speech.
=	(equals sign) Contiguous utterances.
(2.4)	(number in parentheses) Length of a silence.
(.)	(period in parentheses) Micro-pause, 2/10 second or less.
( )	(empty parentheses) Non-transcribable segment of talk.
(word)	(word or phrase in parentheses) Transcriptionist doubt.
((gazing toward the ceiling))	(double parentheses) Description of non-speech activity.

Research on Language and Social Interaction, 32(3), 213–242

Questions, Answers, and the Organization of Talk in the 1992 Vice Presidential Debate: Fundamental Considerations

Jack Bilmes
Department of Anthropology
University of Hawaii

In the 1992 vice presidential debate, the candidates frequently addressed questions to one another. This article, the first of 2, begins a consideration of these questions and the responses they received. It deals with the nature of the candidates' concern with the organization of the talk (which bears directly on their use of and response to questions), the identification of questions and answers and the controversies arising therefrom, and the normative bases for the candidates' practices with regard to questioning and responding to questions. The methodological orientation of this article is that of conversation analysis.

This article is the first of two dealing with the use of questions, and the responses they received, in the 1992 vice presidential debate. The second article will deal in detail with the ways in which questions were presented and placed and the ways in which they were handled by their recipient. This article deals with preliminary matters: the nature of the candidates' concern with the organization of the talk (which bears directly on their use of and response to questions), the identification of questions and answers and the controversies arising therefrom, and the normative bases for the candidates' practices with regard to questioning and re-

Correspondence concerning this article should be sent to Jack Bilmes, Department of Anthropology, University of Hawaii, Honolulu, HI 96826. E-mail: bilmes@hawaii.edu

sponding to questions. This article is less about strategy and tactics as such than about strategic resources. That is, I try to locate the conversational and formal bases for strategic interaction in debates.

Although political debates have been the object of a good deal of academic and journalistic attention, the interactional structure of such debates has not been a primary object of analysis (see Benoit & Wells, 1996, for coverage of previous studies of presidential debates). One does see occasional statements to the effect that a candidate failed to answer a question or respond to an attack. For example, Decker (1990), in an article on the 1988 Quayle–Bentson debate, noted that "the primary characteristic of this debate was that charges and countercharges were made with no real attempt to engage in direct refutation" (p. 172). However, follow-up on such observations typically takes one of two forms—either a general sort of commonsense description ("A said X, and B, instead of responding, talked about Y") or "categorize-and-count." "According to one study of the [Carter–Reagan] debate, Carter's debating style produced twenty-one attacks against Reagan, but only one reply to attacks made by Reagan. In contrast, Reagan attacked Carter sixteen times and replied to Carter's attacks fifteen times" (Ritter & Henry, 1990, p. 82).[1] Another study (Milic, 1979) correlated question types (yes or no, WH [such as where, when], leading, etc.) and candidates' answers (direct, responsive, nonresponsive, evasive or digressive or both).

Perhaps the most elaborate realization of the categorize-and-count approach is that of Benoit and Wells (1996). Their approach, centered as it was on "persuasive attack and defense," might seem inherently interactional. They relied, however, on categorization, subcategorization, and characterization of the content of utterances, and, of course, counting. In contrast, the analytical approach that I adopt concerns itself with the place of utterances in specific interactional contexts, with the ways in which an utterance is enabled by what precedes, defines what is going on, and enables what follows. I consider the ways in which the norms and practices of this form of interaction (i.e., political campaign debate) provide resources for, and constraints on, what can occur at any point, and the ways in which these norms and practices are invoked and used by participants. The focus is on how things work, on process. So, for example, rather than simply classifying a particular response as a member of a preconstituted category, such as "evasion," the analysis is concerned with how the response functions within the sequence of talk in which it occurs. It is these concerns that motivate this article and its forthcoming companion study.

The methodological orientation of this article is that of conversation analysis. Within this tradition, there is only one article that I know of, by Hutchby (1997), that deals with political debate.[2] Hutchby's article is part of a small subliterature in conversation analysis that deals with the relation between speakers and large audiences.[3] Another relevant conversation analysis subliterature is that on broadcast news interviews.[4] Also worthy of special note is Hutchby's (1996) recent book on broadcast confrontational talk. The peculiarities of political campaign debate, as a speech exchange system and as a form of strategic talk, are still largely uninvestigated within conversation analysis.

My subject is the 1992 debate among candidates for the vice presidency of the United States—then Vice President Dan Quayle, then Senator Al Gore, and retired Admiral James Stockdale.[5] In studying the videotape of this debate, I focused on the exchanges between Quayle and Gore, particularly on their use of questions. I chose to analyze this debate because of the many lively exchanges between Gore and Quayle. The speaking style in these exchanges is animated, with much pitch variation, stress, and gesture, conveying intensity and emphasis. (This was true for Gore as well as for Quayle, although Gore's speaking style has been repeatedly characterized in the press as being somewhat wooden.) The exchanges were sharp and confrontational, with frequent overlap.

Debate is not the same as ordinary conversation. It is a special sort of speech exchange system, or, rather, a variety of special sorts. We cannot sufficiently specify what sort of system the 1992 vice presidential debate was by noting that it was a political or even a political campaign debate. The formats of political campaign debates may vary significantly from one occasion to the next. When we look at the specific features of the organization of this debate, it becomes apparent that it is organized in very different ways from ordinary conversation and that these differences are likely to affect what the candidates say.

The moderator began by introducing the candidates and explaining the format of the debate: He explained that, after an opening statement from each candidate—Vice President Quayle, Senator Gore, and Admiral Stockdale—the moderator would raise a series of topics. For each topic, each candidate would get 1 min and 15 sec for a response. Then there would be a 5-min discussion period, during which the candidates might address questions to each other. They would, at the end of the debate, each get 2 min for a closing statement.

We note some of the special features of this form of talk, as it differs from ordinary conversation. First, it is the moderator who sets the topic. Topics in debate are more formal and fixed, more official, than in ordinary conversation, and (in theory) only the moderator can raise them. The speakers must (again, in theory) address the topic raised by the moderator, and only that topic, until the moderator initiates a new topic. As it happens, the moderator sets the topic by asking a question or a number of related questions, which the candidates are to answer in turn. Some of those turns are preallocated and constrained by a specific time limit. There are also, however, "discussion periods," of specified length, when candidates may exchange turns in a more conversational manner. There is also a time limit for the debate itself. Another significant feature of this debate, and debates in general, is that it is for an audience (in this case, both a studio and television audience). It is for the audience, not only in the sense that it is witnessed by the audience but also in the sense that the candidates design their talk for the audience. A political campaign debate is different from an argument in that the objective is not to convince one's interlocutor but to convince the audience and thereby win votes.[6] Finally, I note that the moderator specifically provides for the possibility of the candidates' addressing questions to one another. That this particular speech act (questioning) is singled out within the event itself may suggest to us that it is of special significance.

THE ORGANIZATION OF TALK AS A
TOPIC OF DEBATE

One broad consequence of the debate format, particularly in respect to time limitations and topic handling, is that the candidates manifested strong and explicit concern with the normative and structural properties of the talk. Their concern with questioning and answering as activities (in this debate) was a specific instance of the more general concern with the organization of the talk (in this debate). Much of their debating was about the organization of the debate itself. This concern with organization follows from a strategic regard for control of floor, topic, and interpretation. (The control aspect of the candidates' debate practices is explicit, or at least transparent, in my discussions of their exchanges and is addressed in a more general way in the conclusion to this article.) Some of the structural features they wrangled over were more or less specific to the debating format; others were more generally conversational. Here are a few of many examples. (All transcribed segments, except where otherwise indicated, are from the 1992 vice presidential debate. G stands for Gore, Q for Quayle, and M for the moderator.)

Concern With Fair Distribution of Talk

In lines 05 and 08 of segment (1), in response to Quayle's overlapping talk, Gore invokes a norm of fairness with regard to the distribution and length of turns.

(1)

01	G:		Yeah I- I- I wanna (.) I wanna talk about this because
02			.hhh the question (.) was not about free tra::de (0.5)
03			or education .hh the ⌜question was about lemme- =
04	Q:		⌞Talk about waffling you're=
05	G:	→	=⌜now I let you talk
06	Q:		=⌞the one that brought up the issue of waffling
07			(0.5)
08	G:	→	D:a⌜n let (.) n I let you talk 1- lemme talk now.=
09	Q:		⌞And he's wa:ffled on the abortion issue.
10	G:		='s gonna be a long evening if ya- if y'r like thi:s:
11			now because=[7]

There appears to be an implicit norm that candidates should get approximately the same amount of speaking time.[8] There was also a more specific norm, invoked here, that, when one candidate has had an extended turn at speaking, the other should be accorded the floor for an equally extended turn. The debate moderator may announce or invoke rules regarding fair distribution of talk at the beginning of the debate or during its course, as a way of controlling that distribution. However, as in the above example, rules that are presumed to govern this occasion of talk, including those implicit and general norms grounded in a sense of "fairness," can be invoked by the candidates in contending for the floor or pursuing other tactical aims.

Concern With Interruption

The concern with interruption is, of course, one manifestation of a concern with turn taking. In segment (2), by asking Quayle to let him finish (line 12), Gore is claiming that Quayle's questions (lines 08–09, 11) are interruptive.

```
(2)

01   G:        ... E:ven in ca:ses (.) of rape -and incest (.)th:eir
02             platform (.) requi:res (.) that a woman be penalized (.)
03             that she not be allow:ed to make- a choice (.) if she
04             believes (.) in consultation with her family, .hh or
05             her doctor, (.) ah -and others whoever she chooses (0.5)
06             that (0.8) sh:e wants to have: -an abortion after ra:pe
07             or incest. They make ⌜it completely illegal under any=
08   Q:   →                         ⌞Do you support a twenty four hour
09        →        ⌜waiting period
10   G:        =⌞of those: -circumstances. Now they wanna (.)=
11   Q:   →    ⌜Do you support a twenty four hour waiting period
12   G:        =⌞waffle around on it=let me finish this briefly=Now:
13             (.) now you wanna waffle around on it and give
14             the impre:ssion that maybe you don't really mean what
15             ya say ...
```

This example is quite similar to the first, except that Gore does not rest his claim to the floor on norms of fair distribution of speaking turns. His claim rests simply on the fact that he has the floor and has not finished speaking. Claims of "my turn" and intercessions by the moderator (e.g., "Let him say his thoughts and then you can come in") occur throughout the debate. Although prohibitions on interruption are part of ordinary talk and of very general application, interruption is nevertheless a very frequent occurrence in those political debates that allow direct interchanges among the debaters. In fact, because of a tendency of the candidates to try to maximize their individual speaking time, a certain amount of interruption may be desirable, helping to get the talk equitably distributed. Some of these matters were made explicit by the moderator of a debate between congressional candidates in Hawaii:

> It's okay to interrupt occasionally, especially if the other is lapsing into a minispeech or dodging a specific question, but it's *not* okay to interrupt so often or indiscriminately as to be rude. We want lively exchanges but not ones that deny either candidate a fair chance to weigh in. (Debate between Neil Abercrombie and Orson Swindle, September 22, 1996, on *Price of Paradise* radio program)

Concern With Topic

Quayle's reference to the North American Free Trade Association (NAFTA) agreement in segment (3), line 01, during a discussion whose ostensible topic is abortion, is taken by both the moderator (line 04) and Gore (lines 05–07) to be an improper change of topic.

(3)

```
01  Q:  →   . . . Take the na:fta ((N.A.F.T.A.)) agreement
02  G:      Oh ⌈(***).
03  Q:         ⌊(*) How long how long did he have (***)
04  M:  →   (*) stick to abortion Mister Vice Pre⌈sident.
05  G:  →                                        ⌊I know you
06      →   want to change the subject Dan but let's stick on
07      →   this one for a while
```

A debate is different from ordinary conversation in that, besides the (sub)topics that arise in the course of interaction, there is usually an official topic, set by the moderator. Candidates are supposed to adhere to the topic, and departures from the topic are sanctionable. Of course, that raises as a potential line of contention whether an objected-to utterance was in fact off topic. So, we find Quayle defending himself from the charge of straying from the topic: "Talk about waffling you're the one that brought up the issue of waffling."

Concern With Time Constraints

Unlike ordinary conversation, debates have overall time constraints and frequently, as in this case, time limits on each topic. In segment (4), line 11, after an extended utterance by Gore criticizing President Bush and ending with a question, the moderator announces a change of topic. Unsurprisingly, Quayle expresses a desire to respond to Gore, or at least discomfort at not being allowed to respond (lines 12–13). The moderator refuses to give him time, but mentions that he will have opportunities to respond later (lines 14–15). The moderator can cut off discussion in this way because, as everyone realizes, there are time constraints on the debate and time limits set for each topic within the debate. Quayle implicitly recognizes this by phrasing his objection as a question about the availability of time.

(4)

```
01   G:     ((Recites a list of promises Bush broke and
02          inconsistent statements he made)) . . . Then two weeks
03          ago he said .hh that a- after the election (.) if you
04          win: (.) then (.) James Baker's gonna go back to be
05          Secretary of State .hh Then a week later in the debate:
06          a few nights ago, he said no- after the election if we
07          win .hh James Baker is gonna be in charge of domestic
08          policy. .hh Which is it Dan:=Is he gonna (0.5) a- what's
09          your role in this gonna be.
10          ((Q and audience laugh))
11   M:  →  Well we'll have to move on: to ┌another topic.=
12   Q:  →                                 └(**) I don't have
13          ┌ti- I don't have time to respond to that?
14   M:  →  =└(No) I'm sorry Mr. Vice President (**) You'll get
15       →  plenty of chance to respond so don't worry
```

The moderator's comment that Quayle will have plenty of time to respond is somewhat unrealistic, since the moderator is about to introduce a new topic. The opportunity to respond to a particular point in a conversation, and even more so in a debate, depends on placement as well as time. Quayle will have time to speak eventually, but by that time other matters will be more relevant and pressing. Gore's question, and his attack on Bush, will go unanswered.

Concern With Debate Format

When Gore, in segment (5), after an extended utterance of his own (not shown), cuts Quayle off with a question (line 6), Quayle objects that it is his turn (line 07), invoking perhaps the previously mentioned norm

of fair distribution of speaking turns, as well as a general right to finish
one's utterance without interruption. Gore persists with his question and
Quayle with his resistance. In lines 13 and 17, Gore invokes the rules of
this debate—they are now in the free discussion period. Presumably, he
is questioning Quayle's right to an extended utterance.

```
(5)

01  Q:      A- as our: (.5) family leave act (.) an- because
02          it goes to small businesses where the major problem
03          is .hh your proposal .hh excluded small business
04          that's th- that's the problem.=Now let me talk about
05          health care (* ⌈*)
06  G:  →                 ⌊Did you require it?
07          (0.8)
08  Q:  →   (*) my- ⌈my tur- my- my tur:n
09  G:              ⌊Did you require it?
10          (0.8)
11  Q:      (*)=
12  G:      =Did you requi⌈re (**)
13  M:                    ⌊(* ⌈*)
14  Q:                        ⌊Lighten up Al (.) my turn
15  G:  →   It's a free discussion.
16  Q:      Take a breath Al: Inhale:
17          ((7.0; audience laughter, then applause—G cuts in
18          after .2 second))
19  G:  →   It's a free discussion.
```

Although Gore does not pursue the implications of "free discussion," one
aspect was made clear by the moderator in his opening statement—the
candidates may address questions to one another. However, Gore is not
merely claiming a right to ask a question, he is claiming the right to do
so in a manner that Quayle finds interruptive. The underlying idea here
seems to be that free discussion is to proceed more or less under the rules
of ordinary conversation, where it is, presumably, more acceptable to
insert requests for clarification and elaboration. As we shall see in the
following, there is some specific normative support for Gore's insistence
on inserting his question at this point.

Concern With the Normative Structure of Questioning

Questioning and answering are conversational activities with deep organizational implications. For that reason, debating candidates are concerned not merely with asking and answering questions but with asking and answering as normative activities. Questions, in general, should be answered, and therefore "avoiding the question" is a violation of sorts. In the congressional debate mentioned earlier (in connection with the concern for interruption), the moderator finds interruption justifiable as a way of dealing with a candidate who is "dodging a specific question"; that is, one violation (interruption) is justified as a countermeasure to another violation (evading a posed question). In the following segment, each candidate fails to answer the other's questions, and each protests the failure of the other, accusing him of "avoiding the question."

(6)

```
01  Q:      ... answer my questions.=on the twenny four hour waiting
02          period do you support that?
03  G:      I: have had ⌈the same position on abortion in favor =
04  Q:               ⌊Do you support that?
05  G:      = of a woman's right to choose.=Do you support a
06          woman's ⌈right to choose
07  Q:              ⌊D'you- d'you support a twenny four hour
08          ⌈waiting period (to ha:ve reflection.)
09  G:      ⌊You're still: avoi:ding
10          (.)
11  G:      ⌈you're still avoiding the question.
12  Q:      ⌊Talk about avoi:ding the question.
```

Again, rather than conversing about the topic of abortion, they end up conversing about the topic of conversing. Instead of answering (or simply not answering) each other's questions, they end up talking about a matter of conversational organization, namely, the fact that their questions have not been answered.

Of course, the various concerns listed previously are not really separate. A concern with questioning, for example, necessarily implicates matters of turn taking and topic. When a speaker asks a question, he relinquishes the floor, usually to a specific interlocutor. This gift of the floor, though, comes with burdensome obligations. There is an obligation to accept the "gift." Worse yet, one is constrained to use one's turn to address the subject matter specified by the prior speaker. In what follows, I expand on the normative aspects of questioning and answering, and the tactical implications that ensue from the normative character of those activities.

CONVERSATIONAL NORMS AND THE
IDENTIFICATION OF QUESTIONS AND ANSWERS

The first step in analyzing the use of questions in this debate is to understand the relation of the categories of question and answer to some fundamental rules of questioning and answering. It is the rules that provide for the tactical significance of the categories. Some years ago, I wrote an article (Bilmes, 1988) in which I argued that, although conversation analysis (CA), like pre-Chomskian structural linguistics, used an item-and-arrangement approach, CA was distinctive both in its treatment of "items" (categories of speech) and of rules pertaining to arrangement. Particularly relevant here is the argument concerning categories. In short, categories of speech are not treated in CA as entirely transparent to the analyst. The identity of an item of talk as a particular kind of speech is not fixed at the moment of occurrence. It is subject to claims and counterclaims and so is negotiable. The identification of categories is, in turn, crucial in determining whether particular rules apply to the situation at hand. This point is exemplified and developed in the following examination of how the norms for questioning and answering are related to disputes over the identity of the categories question and answer.

A first norm of questioning (in standard American talk) is that questions call for answers, more or less immediately.[9] An answer is made relevant by the occurrence of a question, and, if it is absent, it will be noticeably missing, an occasion for inference and, possibly, complaint. The problem with failing to answer in debates is not that one has broken a rule and is therefore a bad person; the problem is that not answering may warrant unfavorable inferences. In debate, typically, the inference is that one is evading the question, that to answer would be somehow embarrassing or discreditable or unpopular. The problem, further, is that one is seemingly attempting to hide one's views or actions, a reflection on one's honesty and credibility.[10]

We saw in segment (6) how the "answer questions" norm makes questioning a locus of explicit organizational concern within the debate. Our present interest is in the relation of this norm to the contestation of the categories of question and answer. The existence of the norm, and the possibility of unfavorable inferences resulting from violation of the norm, provides an incentive for certain kinds of contention over the identity of questions and answers in debate. So, for example, a candidate may want to suggest that his opponent did not answer his question, whereas his opponent may want to claim that his reply did constitute an answer. Here is an example from the debate:

(7)

```
01  G:       ... wh:y has (.) George Bush waited for three: and a
02            half years, (.) during this health insurance crisis,
03            .hh before (.) finally coming out with a proposal (.)
04            just before the election (.) and he still: hasn't
05            introduced it in Congress. Why the long wait, Dan.
06            (2.0)
07  M:       Mr. Vice President?
08            (1.0)
09  Q:       Al, (0.8) President Bush has had his health care reform:
10            agenda- on: C:apitol Hill for eight months he's had
11            parts of it up there for years, .hh when you talk about
12            increasing costs the president has had on Capitol Hill
13            (.) medical malpractice reform legislation for several
14            years. .... The president's proposal deals with tax
15            credits, deductions, and purchasing health care in the
16            private sector, and making health care affordable and
17            available to every single American.
.
.             ((transcript skips 7 lines))
.
25  G:   →    We still didn't get an answer to the question of why
26       →    George Bush waited for three and a half yea:rs=
27  Q:   →    =He didn't wait for ⌜three and a half years=I did=
28  G:   →                          ⌞during the national (.)health =
29  Q:   →    =⌜answer the question.
30  G:       =⌞insurance crisis, before he even made a proposal (.)
```

31   and it still hasn't been submitted to Congress- in the
32   form of legislation.

In lines 25 and following, Gore claims that his question, first raised
in lines 01–05, has not been answered. Quayle, in lines 27 and 29, insists
that he has answered, presumably in lines 09–17, which is his only
utterance between Gore's question and Gore's claim that the question
was not answered. The point, then, is not merely theoretical—whether
Quayle has answered Gore's question is a matter of demonstrable interest
to both candidates.

Another way of dealing with a claim that a question has not been
answered, one that I do not have data to illustrate, is to deny that the
relevant utterance was in fact a question. If it was not a question, then
no breach has been committed in not answering.

A reciprocal to the norm that questions call for answers is the
claimable right of the recipient to answer the question immediately on
its occurrence.[11] In segment (8) following, the contention over whether
Quayle has asked a question is understandable in the light of this norm.

(8)

01   Q: . . . the question is 'n' which you have f::ailed to
02   address and that is why is Bill Clinton (0.5) qualified
03   to be president of the United States. .hh You've talked
04   abo⌐ut Jimmy (.) you've talked about Jim Baker =
05   G: →   ⌊Oh I'll be happy to answer (that question).
06   Q: = ((deleted material)) you ⌐haven't told us one=
07   G: →   ⌊I'll be happy to answer=
08   Q: = ⌐reason why Bill Clinton (.) is qualified to be=
09   G: →   = ⌊(*) (.) May I answer(*)?
10   M: ⌊(*) (.) The question (.) was your qualifications.
11   Q: =president ⌐of the United States
12   G: →   ⌊I'll be happy- I'll be happy ⌐(*)
15   Q: ⌊w- I- I
16   wanna go back and make a point (.) ⌐(*)
17   G: →   ⌊Well you've
18   →   asked me a question.=Let me ⌐(*) won't answer my=
19   Q: →   ⌊I (*) I have not asked=
20   G: →   =⌐question I will answer yours.
21   Q: →   =⌊you a question I've made a statement.

22   *((audience laughter. Q cuts in after about one*
23   *second))*
24   Q: →   I have not asked a question I've made a statement that
25   you have not told us why Bill Clinton is qualified
26   (0.5) to be president of the United States.

Gore repeatedly (lines 05, 07, 09, 12, 17–18, 20) tries to answer what he claims is Quayle's question (the claim is explicit in lines 05 and 18). By insisting that Quayle has asked him a question, Gore can claim a right to answer immediately. Quayle, however, denies having asked a question, claiming that the utterance at issue was in fact a statement (lines 19, 21, and 24–26). Therefore, Gore has no immediate right to the floor.

The right-to-answer norm may also be relevant in contention over whether an utterance was or was not an answer. In segment (7), we saw an example of a questioner claiming that his question had not been answered, a claim invested with tactical significance by the answer-questions norm. In the following segment, we see that the party to whom a question has been addressed may also have reason to claim that the question has not been answered. Such a claim may work to his advantage under the right-to-answer norm. This example is drawn from the NAFTA debate between Gore (G) and Ross Perot (P) on the *Larry King* (K) *Show.*

(9) [1993 NAFTA debate]

01   G: . . . well you brought your char:ge t- t'night so I wanna
02   know what speci:fic ⌜changes you would like to make=
03   K: ⌊(***) you're ⌜against it (.)=
04   P: ⌊(*)
05   G: =⌜in the (.) in the treaty.
06   K: =⌊let 'im respo⌜nd (*)
07   P: →   ⌊How can I answer if (.) you keep
08   →   interrupt⌜ing
09   G: →   ⌊Go ahead (*) go ahead
10   (1.0)
11   P: Okay (0.5) no:w (1.0) first (2.0) study thee (.)things
12   that work: the European community (4.0) trade agreement
13   we enter into (0.5) must (.) r:equire he- ah- a social
14   tariff I would say (0.5) that (0.5) m:akes it an even
15   playing field (.) then gives Mexico an incentive to
16   raise the standard of living of its people which it

```
17              does not have now.
18  G:  →  Okay can I ⌈respond now?
19  P:            ⌊(*) standard of living (*)
20  G:      Okay=
21  K:      =Okay ⌈(*)
22  G:  →          ⌊now -so (.) your basic response is- you would
23      →  change it by raising tariffs
24  P:  →  I just started but you interrupted
```

Perot complains in lines 07–08 of being interrupted in his attempt to answer Gore's question, and Gore (line 09) gives him clearance to speak. In line 18, Gore suggests tentatively that the answer has been delivered and it is his turn to respond. Perot does not object, and King seems to accept that it is Gore's turn (line 21). Gore then begins to formulate what he takes to be Perot's answer (lines 22–23), but Perot then objects that his answer was not complete (line 24). This objection has some credibility, because Perot apparently had a list of suggestions, having marked this as his first (line 11). By claiming that he has not yet given his full answer, Perot not only attempts to reclaim the floor but also (in this case, explicitly) suggests that the prior talk was interruptive.

In two-party talk, the possibilities of contestation regarding the identity of questions and answers can be enumerated as follows:

1. A speaker may claim that his utterance was a question, and the other party may deny it. I noted earlier that this possibility is tactically significant under the answer-questions norm, although no actually occurring example was available.
2. A speaker may claim that his utterance was not a question, and the other party may insist it was. This was the situation exemplified in segment (8).
3. A speaker may claim that his utterance was an answer, and the other party may deny it. This is the situation exemplified in segment (7).
4. A speaker may claim that his utterance was not an answer, whereas the other party may hold that it was, as exemplified in segment (9).

It appears, then, that the two norms discussed previously, *answer questions* and *right to answer,* account for the tactical significance of an exhaustive set of possibilities regarding contestation of the identity of questions and answers. (Of course, agreement is the default possibility: In the absence of contestation, agreement is assumed.) These two basic norms of questioning are essential not merely in seeing the tactical significance of the debaters' "moves" but in understanding what they are saying. The argument over whether Quayle asked a question in segment (8), for instance, makes very little sense unless one sees that Gore is invoking a norm that gives him an immediate right of response (see Bilmes, 1986, p. 141, for further discussion of this point). Furthermore, note that the candidates do not argue over the force of the norm itself. They are not disagreeing about whether a question confers a right of immediate response. The validity of the norms is never at issue (in this debate); what is at issue is the applicability of a particular norm to a particular case. Challenging the category membership of particular instances is, however, not the only way of contesting the applicability of a norm to a case. Another way, as we shall see shortly, is to claim that the norm is nullified by a superceding norm.

THE POWER OF QUESTIONS

There is a third norm of questioning that plays a crucial role in this debate. It is obvious that questions are powerful resources for a debater. Through the use of questions, Speaker A can force Speaker B to address A's topic; if B does not do so, he is subject to unfavorable inferences. Yet the power of questions extends beyond the next turn. Sacks (1992, Vol. I) writes that "a person who has asked a question can talk again; has, as we may put it, 'a reserved right to talk again,' after the one to whom he has addressed the question speaks" (p. 264). As stated, this "reserved right" would have consequences only, or at least primarily, in multiparty conversations. I add, though, that it is not just a matter of A asks a question, B speaks, A gets next turn. Rather, A has a right to speak immediately after B answers the question. This, as we shall see, is significantly different from Sacks' formulation. The right of the questioner to speak to an answer and to do so as soon as the answer is complete may be part of a more general rule, the "right of topical response." I propose that when a party produces an utterance on some particular topic, the second party has the right, and sometimes the obligation, to respond on the same topic, and to do so before a new topic is established. Thus, if Speaker A can, by asking a question, obligate B to speak to a certain matter, A will then have the right to speak further to that same matter and may resist any attempt by B to change the topic. Of course, A having responded to B, B will have the same right of response to A. Indeed, it may be the case that, once a topic is ratified (by being spoken to by both parties), it can be properly closed down only by mutual consent, although the consent may consist of nothing more than not resisting a change of topic. That is why discussants can tell each other not to change the topic.

At one point, when Quayle is accused by Gore of talking off topic, he defends himself with "you're the one that brought up the issue of waffling." The rule seems to be that, if A brings up a matter, B may topicalize that matter in the next utterance. B thus has some discretion in deciding what aspect of A's utterance is the topic. A, assuming he accepts B's proposal as to topic, now has the right to respond on that topic, and may properly resist any unilateral attempt by B to change the topic. Thus, a question, insofar as it constrains an answer, opens a topic that is ratified by the answer and thereby initiates an open-ended discussion of the subject.[12]

The aforementioned considerations constitute powerful incentives for debaters to evade or refuse to answer questions on topics that they do not wish to discuss at length, despite the risk of unfavorable inferences. The following exchange illustrates some of the contingencies I have been discussing:

(10)

01	G:		... How can you talk about family values, Dan, (.)and
02			twi:ce (.5) veto: (.) the family medical leave act.
03			((4.0; Applause, overlapped by M and Q))
04	M:		Mr Vice President?
05			(2.0)
06	Q:		A- as our: (0.5) family leave act (.) an- because
07			it goes to small businesses where the major problem
08			is .hh your proposal .hh excluded small business
09		→	that's th- that's the problem.=Now let me talk about
10		→	health care (* ⌐*)
11	G:	→	⌊Did you require it? (0.8)
12	Q:	→	(*) my- ⌐my tur- my- my tur:n
13	G:		⌊Did you require it?

```
14              (0.8)
15   Q:         (*)=
16   G:         =Did you requi⌐re (**)
17   M:                  └(*⌐*)
18   Q:                     └Lighten up Al (.) my turn
19   G:    →    It's a free discussion.
20   Q:         Take a breath Al: Inhale:
21              ((7.0; audience laughter, then applause—G cuts in
22              after .2 second))
23   G:         It's a free discussion.
24              ((laughter continues—G cuts in again))
25   G:         Did you require: (1.5) did you require family leave in
26              that legislation yes or no.
27   Q:         We requ- we offered incentives to small
28              businesses, (.) Yes or no (.) ⌐were small busines-=
29   G:                                       └(**)
30   Q:    →    =wer- were small business exempted under your
31         →    proposal?
32   G:    →    Yes.
33   Q:    →    Yes and that's where the big (est pro⌐blem **)
34   G:    →                                         └Did you
35              require it of anyone?
36              (0.5)
37   Q:    →    I'm gonna get back to the topic ⌐(*) because he=
38   G:                                          └Did you require
39              it of anyone.
40   Q:         =obviously doesn't wanna talk about health
41              insurance or health care which you ((the
42              moderator)) .hh a: a- address . . .
```

Gore (lines 01–02) asks a question, and Quayle (lines 06–10) offers a reply and then attempts to move on to another topic. He leaves no pause whatsoever between his answer and his new topic. This suggests that he is aware that Gore may attempt to comment on his answer and that he is trying to prevent this by getting his new topic underway before Gore can speak. Gore, for his part, withholds his talk until it becomes apparent that Quayle has completed his answer and is moving on to a new topic. At that point, he raises a question on the old topic (line 11). The structure of this sequence is not adequately represented as question–answer–question. It is, rather, question–answer–response to answer (which happens to be another question). Only if we see it this way can we understand why Gore can claim the right to interrupt Quayle as he does.[13]

Quayle resists answering Gore's "Did you require it?," first on the basis that it is his turn and so Gore's question is out of order (lines 12, 18). (Quayle implicitly invokes a notion of fair play; Gore, having had an extended, uninterrupted turn at talk, should give Quayle the same.) If Gore has no right to speak, he has no right to ask a question, and so Quayle is not obliged to answer. Gore persists, and counters by pointing out that they are in a "free discussion" (lines 19, 23), with no preallotted turns. Gore's persistence suggests that he has a strong sense of his right to interrupt Quayle in this instance. Free discussion, however, does not confer an unlimited right of interruption; it is Quayle's turn not only by virtue of a fair distribution norm but also by virtue of the fact that he had the floor and had not finished speaking. Gore is implicitly invoking a right of topical response by his insistence on responding to Quayle's answer in lines 06–10 before the topic is changed. Quayle then turns the right of topical response to his own advantage by asking Gore a question (lines 29–30).

One way to at least temporarily avoid answering a question is to respond with a question of one's own. There are, I think, limitations to this tactic—not just any second question will do. However, one maneuver that seems to be legitimate is to ask the original questioner to answer a question of the same type as the one he has asked. The underlying notion is that one should not ask a question that oneself would be unwilling to answer. Gore answers immediately and unambiguously (line 32). It is noteworthy that he does so in the briefest possible way, with a single word. To offer a more elaborate answer would be to invite topicalization of the Democratic legislation or to risk some ambiguity or incompleteness that Quayle could use to construct another question. Nevertheless, Quayle then, instead of answering Gore's question, comments on Gore's answer (line 33). Quayle uses the same tactic that Gore has been using to extend a question–answer sequence. Gore does not take the bait and returns to his own question (lines 34–35), overlapping Quayle's comment. (Quayle might have put more pressure on Gore by asking a follow-up question instead of making an assertive comment.) At this point, Quayle invokes another norm. He is going to "get back to the topic." That is, he is going to speak, as required, to the topic raised by the moderator.

It is my feeling that Quayle has not "played fair" here. This feeling is, I think, based on another normative aspect of questioning. Sacks (1992,

Vol. II) said, "Not any question can follow a question, and the questions
that can lawfully follow a question are insertion sequences. And, roughly,
an insertion sequence's questions are such questions as propose 'If you
answer this one I will answer yours' " (p. 528).[14] I suggest the following
corollary: When B responds to A's question with a question, B is proposing, by virtue of having asked the question, that his question is
legitimate ("lawful"). Therefore, B is proposing that, if A answers his
question, B will answer A's question.[15] In other words, when Quayle asks
his question in lines 30–31, there is an implicit commitment that, if Gore
answers, Quayle will answer Gore's prior question.

Quayle ultimately refuses to answer Gore's question, although it is
by now quite clear what the answer would have to be. Nevertheless, by
not offering an answer, he avoids topicalizing the matter. Whether his
approach is strategically sound is arguable. Although he has avoided
having to discuss a possible weak point in Bush's proposed legislation,
he has not only visibly failed to answer a question, but his refusal has
also provoked an extended exchange. Having failed to deter Gore by
claiming the turn, he finally develops the implication of his lines 09–10;
he will not answer because Gore's question is not on topic. He is going
to "get back to the topic," which is health care. Gore, he claims, does
not want to talk about this, and so, it is implied, it is Gore who is really
avoiding the question.

There are at least six norms of talk that are relevant to the struggle
in segment (10) for control of the talk:

1. Answer questions.
2. Fair or proper distribution of turns and allotment of floor time.
3. Right to complete utterance, uninterrupted.
4. Right of topical response.
5. Candidates should stay on the topic set by the moderator.
6. Asking a question in answer to a question generally involves a
   commitment to answer the first question, if the second is answered,
   especially when the second question is similar to the first.

It has already been noted that the candidates never contest the validity
of the norms as such. Instead, challenges are made to the applicability
of the norm to this particular situation. One way that this can be done,
as was illustrated in the preceding section, is by contesting the categorization of items of speech. Another way, as we have seen in this section,

is by advancing some other norm as having priority. So, a question, with its inherent demand for an answer, can be neutralized by pointing out that it is off topic.

INTERACTIONAL RHETORIC

Rhetoric is, in its classical sense, the art of influencing the thought and conduct of one's hearers by means of persuasive language.[16] Clearly, the candidates in this or any political campaign debate are engaging in a form of rhetoric. When we think about rhetoric, we are likely to consider such matters as choice of words, figures of speech, enthymemes, style of delivery, or the five traditional "departments" of rhetoric—invention, arrangement, style, memory, and delivery. We are likely to think of rhetoric as essentially monological. Studies of rhetoric, that is to say, have dealt with utterances, spoken or written, not with interaction. This is not to say that there is never any mention of interactional matters. Still, it is apparent that the overwhelming concern of rhetorical study has been with language (and sometimes other channels of communication, such as gesture, posture, and dress) rather than with dialogue. However, there is an interactional component to debates, and, because this is interaction for an audience, the speaker must attend to the effect produced by his style of interaction. A speaker may present a well-formed and perfectly delivered argument on an issue of crucial importance, and yet his speech may be judged inadequate because it fails to address the question or challenge that his opponent has just put before him.[17] What seems, in isolation, a perfectly reasonable piece of talk may, in context, appear evasive or obtuse. Again, a debater may be judged too aggressively interruptive, or too timid, or too intolerant of interruption. Furthermore, part of the skill of unstructured debate[18] consists in the ability to compete with one's opponent for the floor, for clear stretches of speaking time.[19] This, it seems to me, is reasonably treated as a fundamental rhetorical skill.

The debater is in a situation in which, although he is interacting for an audience, he is not, for the most part, interacting with the audience. On the one hand, he needs to communicate in a specific way with his audience, but, on the other hand, his audience expects him to be responsive to his opponent and follow the usual norms of interaction (as modified by the debate format). Also, his opponent will try to shape that interaction, insofar as this is possible, so as to impede his free communication with the audience. He must handle these contingencies within the specific time constraints of a formal debate. These time constraints accentuate a feature of ordinary conversation—if a matter is currently relevant and you do not speak to it now, you may not have the opportunity to speak to it later.[20] This feature is a resource as well as a problem for the debater, because he may employ tactics to prevent his opponent from speaking freely. These tactics, too, are part of the subject matter of interactional rhetoric.

CONCLUSION

We return to the observation that the candidates display a strong and persistent concern with the organization of the talk. We are now in a position to begin to answer two questions regarding that concern: Why are they so interested in organizational matters?, and Their interest being a practical one, what resources can they bring to bear in attempting to influence the organization of the talk?

The debater is in a peculiar position. He is trying to sway the audience, not his debate opponents. Nevertheless, he must attend to his opponents, he must interact with them, or he will not be seen as debating. The relative emphasis given to these two objectives, communicating with the audience as he wishes and interacting "properly" with his opponents, and the methods used to achieve these objectives, are crucial aspects of debating strategy. It is the constraints that interaction places on communication with an audience, and the mutual attempt to exploit these constraints vis-à-vis one's opponent within the time limitations of a debate, that explain the candidates' pervasive concern with the organization of the talk. This can be seen more clearly by examining specific issues of control.

There are at least three control issues: (a) Who has the floor and for how long, (b) what can be said and on what topic, and (c) how are utterances to be interpreted. The first issue is one of time. Whoever has the most speaking time has the greatest opportunity to present arguments and influence the audience. Also, in periods of "free discussion," the time in which A monopolizes the floor is time in which B cannot speak. Candidates may, for example, maximize the length of their own turns and interrupt their opponents' turns. However, norms of fair play and politeness constrain these tactics. Just as there are incentives to transgress the usual norms of conversational organization, there are incentives for one's opponent to point out and resist these transgressions with claims such as "my turn" and demands such as "let me finish."

Control of topic is another organizational matter of great concern to the candidates.[21] Each candidate has a number of topics to which he would particularly like to speak and a number that he would prefer to avoid. This fact implicates tactics both of asking and answering. One wants to answer questions in a way that appears responsive but at the same time avoids areas of weakness. This is a delicate matter, as one must appear to be answering the question asked on pain of being seen as evasive. Also, such techniques are vulnerable to follow-up questions. Questions are the primary instruments for controlling the topic beyond one's own immediate turn. Again, debaters do not simply rely on the audience to notice violations of norms of topical consistency. They pressure and sanction one another with expressions such as "stick to the subject," "I'm still waiting to hear the answer," and "you're avoiding the question." As illustrated in segment (10), "getting back to the topic" can also be used as a warrant for not answering a posed question.

Finally, there is the matter of controlling interpretation. One of the lessons of recent work on conversation is that utterances do not have an inherent and final meaning at the instant they are produced. Their meaning is subject to negotiation. They mean what they ultimately come to mean (Bilmes, 1988; Schegloff, 1984; Streeck, 1980). The particular significance of this fact, insofar as our present interests are concerned, is that an utterance's status as a speech act may be arguable. More specifically, there may be disagreement as to whether a particular utterance is or is not a question, or as to whether it is or is not an answer. Because of the norms governing questioning, this is a matter of some import. The audience's perception of a participant's conversational rights and responsibilities may hinge on the plausibility of a proffered interpretation, and it is the norms of conversational organization that make the interpretation of an utterance as a certain type of speech act so crucial.

Underlying and in part constituting the talk we have examined is a complex arrangement of claimed and claimable rights, obligations, understandings, and expectations regarding the organization of that talk. These normative elements are used to negotiate aspects of the conversational organization, as when a normatively based claim to an extended turn at talk is opposed by an appeal to free discussion, or an attempt to follow up on a question is negated by a call to return to "the topic," or a demand for an answer (normatively required by the asking of a question) is deemed illegitimate by virtue of the question's being improperly placed. Also, the invocation of a norm may raise issues regarding the identity of constituent elements (as when the demand to be allowed to answer a question raises the issue of whether a question has been asked). These normative elements do not govern the talk in any simple sense; rather, they provide the means for negotiating the organization of the talk on the spot (Bilmes, 1976) and, because much of the talk is about organization, of making sense of that talk.

NOTES

1 Ritter and Henry (1990) provided some "supporting" evidence that raises troubling questions about this form of analysis. "Another study revealed the same trend, reporting that Carter responded to only about 25 percent of the charges made by Reagan" (p. 82). Note that the first study they cited had Carter responding to only 1 of 16 attacks. The security of the statistics is undermined by the indeterminacy of the categorization process.

2 Another article (Beck, 1996) has recently come to my attention, which is not only about debate and in the conversation analytic tradition but also is specifically about the 1992 vice presidential debate. There are, as might be expected, some points of commonality between that article and this one, but the redundancy is not great and the analyses are largely distinct.

3 See, for example, Atkinson (1984a, 1984b, 1985), Heritage and Greatbatch (1986), and Clayman (1993a).

4 See, for example, Heritage (1985), Greatbatch (1986a, 1986b, 1988, 1992), Clayman (1988, 1991, 1992, 1993b), Heritage and Greatbatch (1991), and Heritage and Roth (1995).

5 I know of only one other academic study of this debate, by Carlin and Bicak (1993), which is a highly subjective evaluation of the participants' performances in terms of the purposes that the authors conceive should be furthered by a vice presidential debate.

6 *Convince* may not be precisely the right word for what the candidate is trying to do. He is trying to favorably impress the audience and to create an unfavorable impression of his opponent.

7   The transcript segments use standard conversation analytic transcription conventions, with two additions. Each asterisk in parenthesis (*) represents approximately ½ sec of speech that the analyst has been unable to transcribe, and a hyphen immediately preceding a word indicates "new articulation" rather than a connected glide from the previous sound.

8   At a couple of points in the Gore–Perot North American Free Trade Association debate, the moderator assures Perot that he is monitoring the time and that both debaters have had the floor for equal amounts of time.

9   It has been noted that the rule calling for immediate answers to questions does not seem to be in effect for at least some occasions of talk among certain American Indians (Philips, 1983). Spindler (1963) claimed that even "asking direct questions [among the Menomini Indians] is distasteful" (p. 361).

10 Although not answering a question is always meaningful, the inferences consequent on not answering are not necessarily unfavorable. In the course of Gore's opening statement, the following occurs:

> 01   G: . . . I'll make you a deal this evening. If you don't try
> 02   to compare George Bush to Harry Truman, I won't
> 03   compare you to Jack Kennedy. ((*laughter from audience*
> 04   *and from Quayle*))
> 05   G: Harry ⌈Truman
> 06   Q: ⌊You remember the last time someone compared
> 07   themself to Jack Kennedy? You remember what they said?
> 08   (2.0)
> 09   G: Harry Truman is worth remembering . . .

Gore has rather obviously neglected to answer Quayle's questions. However, arguably, this is an embarrassment for Quayle rather than Gore because Gore, by not answering, highlights the fact that Quayle has spoken out of turn.

11 Sacks, Schegloff, and Jefferson (1974) wrote, "If the turn-so-far is so constructed as to involve the use of a 'current speaker selects next' technique, then the party so selected has rights, and is obliged, to take the next turn to speak, and no others have such rights or obligations, transfer occurring at that place" (p. 704). They may have made their point too powerfully—see Power and Martello (1986)—but the turn transfer should occur at, at least, approximately that place.

12 In G. B. Shaw's *Village Wooing* (1987), a male character complains, "It is your privilege as a woman to have the last word. Please take it and don't end all your remarks with a question" (p. 320). The problem here is not that the woman is extending the conversation by one turn, giving him the last word. The problem is that she is extending it indefinitely because she may respond to any answer that he gives, and her response may incorporate a further question.

13 A similar sequence occurs at another point in the debate:

```
01  G:  Isn't it a fa:ct Da:n (.) that every single one of those
02      ess ess ((SS)) eighteens is still there, .hh in the silos:
03      and under the start one treaty, .hh only ha:lf of
04      the silos are supposed to be dismantled, (.) ┌and=
05  Q:                                              └Sa-
06  G:  =there is no deal (.) to get rid of the other half. =
07      =Didn't the president make a mistake ┌here
08  Q:                                       └(The president)
09  G:  ┌(**)
10  M:  └(*) Vice President Quayle ┌(please)
11  Q:                            └The president does have
12      a commitment from Boris Yeltsin to: eliminate the
13      ess ess eighteens .hh that is a commitment ┌to:
14  G:                                             └Is it
15      an agreement?
16  Q:  It is a commitment: a:nd u: (.) we ┌had w- w- it's it =
17  G:                                     └a- oh::
18  Q:  =is a (0.8) Well let's let's ta- let's- let's- let's ta- let's-
19      let's talk abou:t (.) ┌let's let's talk abou:t let's ta
20  G:                        └Well he said it's done ┌(*)
21  M:                                                └Let
22      him let him talk senator
23  Q:  s lighten up here Al
24      ((3.0, audience laughter. M speaks halfway
25      through))
26  M:  uh (.) Go ahead
27      (1.0)
28  Q:  Let's- let's ta- let's ta:lk abou:t (.) getting (.)
29      agreements. . . .
```

Gore overlaps Quayle at line 14, to follow up on his original question, which Quayle has not specifically answered. In line 20, at the very point where Quayle makes it apparent that he is going to change the subject, Gore inserts a comment. On this occasion, the moderator intervenes on Quayle's behalf. One reason for this may be that the question has been implicitly answered—Quayle has admitted that it is a commitment, not an agreement. Gore is not trying to add or elicit further information but simply to drive the point home. Perhaps more important, the situation has become unseemly—Gore is baiting Quayle, who has lost his ability to speak articulately.

14 Also, Levinson (1983):

> Given a first part of a pair, a second part is immediately relevant and expectable (Schegloff, 1972, p. 363ff). If such a second fails to occur, it is noticeably absent; and if some other first part occurs in its place then that will be heard where possible as some preliminary to the doing of the second part. (p. 306)

15 There are exceptions to the general expectation that the asker of a second-position question is, if he gets an answer, obliged to answer the original question. For example, "You don't expect me to answer that, do you?" There are probably quite a few exceptions. I propose this "norm" in a tentative and unelaborated fashion as a possible explanation for my sense that Quayle is not playing fair.

16 "Aristotle defines rhetoric as *the art or faculty of discovering the best possible means of persuasion in regard to any subject whatever*" (Winterowd, 1968, p. 14). "Rhetoric is public utterance . . . designed to produce an effect of some kind" (Nichols, 1974, p. 180).

17 When respondents were asked to explain the factors that influenced their judgments of the October 11, 1992, presidential debate and the October 13, 1992, vice presidential debate, specificity of response to posed questions was, respectively, the second and fourth most mentioned item (Winkler & Black, 1993, p. 79).

18 A debate, in my usage, is unstructured to the degree that it allows ordinary conversational give-and-take, rather than fixed turns controlled by the moderator.

19 Level of participation was the second most mentioned factor offered by respondents in explaining their judgments of the 1992 vice presidential debate (Winkler & Black, 1993, p. 79). The fact that this factor was more noticeable in the vice presidential than in the presidential debate may have to do with the presence in the former of Admiral Stockdale, who had relatively little to say. Also, time was more formally allotted in the presidential debates, whereas the vice presidential debate provided for "free discussion."

20 See, for example, Jefferson (1986, p. 160). Sacks (1992) put it this way: "If you had something to say at point X, then it could very shortly be that you would have to say something very different, to be saying something understandably" (Vol. I, p. 527).

21 I am using *topic* very broadly, to mean "what is being talked about." The general subject of abortion, for example, is a topic, but so is "Gore's position on parental notification."

REFERENCES

Atkinson, J. M. (1984a). *Our masters' voices: The language and body language of politics.* London: Methuen.

Atkinson, J. M. (1984b). Public speaking and audience response: Some techniques for inviting applause. In J. M. Atkinson & J. Heritage (Eds.), *Structures of social action:*

Studies in conversation analysis (pp. 370–409). Cambridge, England: Cambridge University Press.

Atkinson, J. M. (1985). Refusing invited applause: Preliminary observations from a case study of charismatic oratory. In T. A. van Dijk (Ed.), *Handbook of discourse analysis* (Vol. 3, pp. 161–181). New York: Academic.

Beck, C. (1996). "I've got some points I'd like to make here": The achievement of social face through turn management during the 1992 vice presidential debate. *Political Communication, 13,* 165–180.

Benoit, W. L., & Wells, W. T. (1996). *Candidates in conflict: Persuasive attack and defense in the 1992 presidential debates.* Tuskaloosa: University of Alabama Press.

Bilmes, J. (1976). Rules and rhetoric: Negotiating the social order in a Thai village. *Journal of Anthropological Research, 32,* 44–57.

Bilmes, J. (1986). *Discourse and behavior.* New York: Plenum.

Bilmes, J. (1988). Category and rule in conversation analysis. *Papers in Pragmatics, 2,* 25–59.

Carlin, D. B., & Bicak, P. J. (1993). Toward a theory of vice presidential debate purposes: An analysis of the 1992 vice presidential debate. *Argumentation and Advocacy, 30,* 119–130.

Clayman, S. (1988). Displaying neutrality in television news interviews. *Social Problems, 35,* 474–492.

Clayman, S. (1991). News interview openings: Aspects of sequential organization. In P. Scannell (Ed.), *Broadcast talk: A reader* (pp. 48–75). Newbury Park, CA: Sage.

Clayman, S. (1992). Footing in the achievement of neutrality: The case of news interview discourse. In P. Drew & J. Heritage (Eds.), *Talk at work* (pp. 163–198). Cambridge, England: Cambridge University Press.

Clayman, S. (1993a). Booing: The anatomy of a disaffiliative response. *American Sociological Review, 58,* 110–130.

Clayman, S. (1993b). Reformulating the question: A device for answering/not answering questions in news interviews and press conferences. *Text, 13,* 159–188.

Debate between Neil Abercrombie and Orson Swindle (S. Roth, Director). (1996). In S. Roth (Producer), *Price of Paradise.* Honolulu: KHPR.

Decker, W. D. (1990). The 1988 Quayle–Bentson vice presidential debate. In R. V. Friedenberg (Ed.), *Rhetorical studies of national political debates* (pp. 167–185). New York: Praeger.

Greatbatch, D. L. (1986a). Aspects of topical organization in news interviews: The use of agenda shifting procedures by interviewees. *Media, Culture and Society, 8,* 441–455.

Greatbatch, D. L. (1986b). Some standard uses of supplementary questions in news interviews. In J. Wilson & B. Crow (Eds.), *Belfast working papers in language and linguistics, Vol. 8* (pp. 86–123). Jordanstown, Northern Ireland: University of Ulster.

Greatbatch, D. L. (1988). A turn-taking system for British news interviews. *Language in Society, 17,* 401–430.

Greatbatch, D. L. (1992). The management of disagreement between news interviewees. In P. Drew & J. Heritage (Eds.), *Talk at work* (pp. 268–301). Cambridge, England: Cambridge University Press.

Heritage, J. (1985). Analyzing news interviews: Aspects of the production of talk for an overhearing audience. In T. A. van Dijk (Ed.), *Handbook of discourse analysis, Vol. 3* (pp. 95–119). New York: Academic.

Heritage, J., & Greatbatch, D. (1986). Generating applause: A study of rhetoric and response at party political conferences. *American Journal of Sociology, 19,* 110–157.

Heritage, J., & Greatbatch, D. (1991). On the institutional character of institutional talk: The case of news interviews. In D. Boden & D. H. Zimmerman (Eds.), *Talk and social structure* (pp. 93–137). Berkeley: University of California Press.

Heritage, J. C., & Roth, A. L. (1995). Grammar and institution: Questions and questioning in the broadcast news interview. *Research on Language and Social Interaction, 28,* 1–60.

Hutchby, I. (1996). *Confrontation talk: Arguments, asymmetries, and power on talk radio.* Mahwah, NJ: Lawrence Erlbaum Associates, Inc.

Hutchby, I. (1997). Building alignments in public debate: A case study from British TV. *Text, 17,* 1–20.

Jefferson, G. (1986). Notes on "latency" in overlap onset. *Human Studies, 9,* 153–183.

Levinson, S. C. (1983). *Pragmatics.* Cambridge, England: Cambridge University Press.

Milic, L. T. (1979). Grilling the pols: Q and A at the debates. In S. Kraus (Ed.), *The great debates: Carter versus Ford, 1976* (pp. 187–208). Bloomington: Indiana University Press.

Nichols, M. H. (1974). Rhetoric and the humane tradition. In W. R. Fisher (Ed.), *Rhetoric: A tradition in transition* (pp. 178–191). East Lansing: Michigan State University Press.

Philips, S. U. (1983). *The invisible culture: Communication in classroom and community on the Warm Springs Indian Reservation.* Prospect Heights, IL: Waveland.

Power, R. J. D., & Martello, M. F. D. (1986). Some criticisms of Sacks, Schegloff, and Jefferson on turn taking. *Semiotica, 58,* 29–40.

Ritter, K., & Henry, D. (1990). The 1980 Reagan–Carter presidential debate. In R. V. Friedenberg (Ed.), *Rhetorical studies of national political debates* (pp. 69–93). New York: Praeger.

Sacks, H. (1992). *Lectures on conversation (Vols. I & II).* Edited by G. Jefferson. Oxford, England: Blackwell.

Sacks, H., Schegloff, E. A., & Jefferson, G. (1974). A simplest systematics for the organization of turn-taking for conversation. *Language, 50,* 696–735.

Schegloff, E. A. (1972). Sequencing in conversational openings. In J. J. Gumperz & D. Hymes (Eds.), *Directions in sociolinguistics* (pp. 346–380). New York: Holt, Rinehart & Winston.

Schegloff, E. A. (1984). On some questions and ambiguities in conversation. In J. M. Atkinson & J. Heritage (Eds.), *Structures of social action: Studies in conversation analysis* (pp. 28–52). Cambridge, England: Cambridge University Press.

Shaw, G. B. (1987). *Village wooing.* In *Bernard Shaw: Selected short plays* (pp. 317–342). Middlesex, England: Penguin.

Spindler, G. D. (1963). Personality, sociocultural system, and education among the Menomini. In G. D. Spindler (Ed.), *Education and culture: Anthropological approaches* (pp. 351–399). New York: Holt, Rinehart & Winston.

Streeck, J. (1980). Speech acts in interaction: A critique of Searle. *Discourse Processes, 3,* 133–154.

Winkler, C. K., & Black, C. F. (1993). Assessing the 1992 presidential and vice presidential debates: The public rationale. *Argumentation and Advocacy, 30,* 77–87.

Winterowd, W. R. (1968). *Rhetoric: A synthesis.* New York: Holt, Rinehart & Winston.

Research on Language and Social Interaction, 32(3), 243–267
Copyright © 1999, Lawrence Erlbaum Associates, Inc.

Rhetorical Strategies in Audience Participation Debates on Radio and TV

Ian Hutchby
Department of Human Sciences
Brunel University

In this article I analyze the talk of lay contributors in TV and radio variants of audience participation shows. Lay contributors use their initial occupancy of the floor to produce turns in which they take up positions, or argue with others' positions, on an issue. I explore some key rhetorical devices and strategies (understood as techniques of "artifice or finesse") used by lay contributors in making their cases. I discuss the ways in which a particular set of rhetorical forms functions as a format for achieving completeness in an extended audience-directed utterance, and thereby help to coordinate lay contributors' points and the studio audience's response to what has been said. I show that ordinary citizens speaking in the situations provided by audience participation debate shows can be just as adept at using effective rhetorical devices as are more seasoned public speakers, and moreover, that they are able to do so in improvised, rather than previously written, discourse.

Audience participation debate shows on radio and TV provide a public arena in which private citizens can express their opinions on issues in the public domain.[1] A central part of the institutionalized format of such shows involves members of the public being invited by the host to have their say on particular matters of concern. One upshot of this is that

Correspondence concerning this article should be sent to Ian Hutchby, Department of Human Sciences, Brunel University, Uxbridge, Middlesex UB8 3PH, United Kingdom. E-mail: ian.hutchby@brunel.ac.uk

we might consider these shows as contexts in which the talk is strategic in a particular sense. *Chambers Twentieth Century Dictionary* (MacDonald, 1981) defines *strategy* in two ways: as "generalship, or the art of conducting a campaign and manoeuvring an army" and as "artifice or finesse generally" (p. 1335). Although it is the first sense that informs much thinking about strategic action, it is in the second of these senses that I think talk on audience participation debate shows can be described as strategic. These shows represent contexts in which lay speakers marshal various resources of talk-in-interaction to put forward an argument, take up a stance, and make a point about some specific issue, in interaction with professional broadcasters (hosts) and often, also, large-scale copresent audiences. When we examine the ways in which those arguments are constructed, we find a great deal of "artifice and finesse" in the form of lay speakers' mastery of a range of rhetorical devices.

The following analysis focuses on the talk of lay contributors in both TV and radio variants of audience participation shows. My data are drawn from two principal sources: a collection of recordings of a talk radio show, *The Brian Hayes Show,* gathered between 1988 and 1989 in London, England;[2] and an episode of the U.S. TV talk show *Oprah Winfrey* (HARPO Productions), originally broadcast in 1991, in which the Rodney King police brutality case is discussed by audience members and representatives of the Chicago Police Department.[3] In both these settings, members of the public are routinely provided with the space to have their say, often at some length, on matters under discussion.[4] However, there are some key differences between the two types of settings. Talk radio typically involves single speakers (callers) interacting with the show's regular host (and possibly also a studio guest such as a spokesperson or expert on the main issue of the day). The TV variant, on the other hand, involves audience participants speaking from within a relatively large studio audience, interacting with both the host and the invited guests or experts whose task it frequently is to put or defend an official line on the key issue. Perhaps the major difference here is that in the latter setting audience speakers routinely attract responses to what they say, usually in the form of clapping or jeering, from the other members of the studio audience, whereas on talk radio, the only broadcast response to a caller's opinions comes from the host.

These differences aside, one basic similarity between the two formats is that audience members (in TV shows) or callers (on talk radio) routinely use their initial occupancy of the floor to produce turns in which they take up positions, or argue with others' positions, on an issue. In other words, lay speakers focus on presenting their opinions immediately on being given an invitation to speak by the host. My aim in this article is to explore the rhetorical devices, or strategies in the second sense mentioned above, used by lay contributors in making their cases. In pursuit of this, two related issues are discussed, both of which can be taken to be high in contextual relevance for the participants. First, on both talk radio and talk TV, the lay contributor typically can be assured of only one opportunity to make their point (others may occur, but only one is actually ensured). This opportunity comes when the host begins, as is typically the case (see Hutchby, 1996), by asking them to state their views. There are thus good reasons why the speaker may wish, having been given the chance to make their point, actually to ensure that they get their point in in the one chance they can count on having. In the first part of the article I describe two main variants of a common rhetorical format that speakers use in order to achieve completeness for their arguments.

The second issue is more specifically related to the TV versions that involve a copresent studio audience. In this setting, as noted, lay speakers frequently receive applause for their contributions. Drawing on Atkinson's (1984) well-known work analyzing the rhetorical forms involved in coordinating audience applause with the salient points in a platform speaker's oration, I discuss the ways in which similar forms function—in combination with the format for achieving completeness—in coordinating lay contributors' points and the studio audience's response to what has been said. We thus see how ordinary citizens speaking in the situations provided by audience participation debate shows can be just as adept at using these rhetorical devices as the more seasoned public speakers in Atkinson's data.

PRODUCING A "COMPLETE" ARGUMENT

One of the most characteristic sequential environments in which lay speakers take the floor on talk radio and talk TV is following an invitation of some form by the host or moderator. There are other places in which lay participants speak—for instance, if they are engaging in arguments with other participants—but in this article I focus exclusively on these invited turns which I call *opinion presentations*.

Thornborrow (1997) showed that lay speakers' contributions can take a variety of forms, from single sentence aphorisms such as "I think all police think black people look alike" (see extract [2] later), to extended stories recounting some personal experience. Yet whatever form they take, Thornborrow argued that the turns function as position-taking contributions in the debate. Thus, even stories that appear simply to recount a set of events without overtly making a point can be treated by other participants as implicating a point and situating the speaker in relation to the issue under discussion. If we focus purely on the initial opinion presentations, however, things appear slightly different in the sense that lay speakers typically are concerned to round off or emphasize the point of their opinion presentations using certain identifiable rhetorical formats and devices. In other words, as I show presently, opinion presentations are structured to be "complete" (though whether that completeness is recognized or not by recipients is another matter).

This in turn is related to a particular sequential issue. Given that these turns are produced in an environment where the speaker is being given the floor to have their say in a more or less extended turnspace, there is the question of coordination between the completion of the opinion presentation and the onset of a response (whether that response comes in the form of an utterance from a particular next speaker or a collective burst of applause). In the context of talk radio and talk TV shows, shorter opinion presentations consisting of only one or two turn-constructional units can prove problematic on this count. For instance, extract (1) comes from a talk radio call. Having been introduced, the caller takes just a single sentence to state his view on the question of "whether the Queen should go on a state visit to Russia":

(1) [Talk Radio]

```
1   Host:    Gary no:w, frum Barnet.
2   Caller:  .hh Yeah hello. I don't see the problem with the Queen
3            going tuh Russia at a:ll.
4            (2.1)
5   Host:    Mm?
6   Caller:  I mean e- I've- we(h) heh uh- I don't understa:nd . . .
7            ((goes on to offer justification))
```

This opinion presentation gets no response for over 2 sec, until the host indicates, with "Mm?," that he expects the caller to say more. The caller orients to that as a requirement to furnish some justification for his view, which he goes on to provide.

When an audience is present, as in talk TV debates, an additional feature is that the audience applauds (or otherwise manifests a response to) what individual speakers have to say. As we will see later, there are rhetorical devices available by which speakers may manage the occurrence of this applause. However, in single sentence opinion presentations, there may again prove to be problems for those who want to react to the speaker's view:

(2) [*Oprah Winfrey Show*]

```
1  Oprah:     What do you say.
2             (1.5)
3  Man:       I think that uh, all police think black people look
4             alike.
5  Oprah:     Mm hmm.
6             (1.1)
7  Oprah:     And ⌐what do you think
8  Audience:     └x-xx-xxx-x-xxx-
```

In the above extract, the host responds simply by saying "Mm hmm" (line 5). Subsequently there is a 1.1-sec gap during which the audience member says nothing more, and Oprah moves on to address another contributor. The audience in fact applauds the first speaker's opinion, but only after the pause, once it is clear that Oprah has treated the man's contribution as complete by moving on. The applause itself is only weak and sporadic.

By contrast, consider the following extract:

(3) [*Oprah Winfrey Show*]

```
1  Oprah:     You say what ma'am?
2  Woman:     I say that thee, u:h report that's sitting on
3             Superintendent Martin's desk which is, he's thee: head
4             of thee oaf- Officer Professional Standards which is the
5             internal police investigative body, .hh o:nly goe:s, .h
6             tuh his desk, .h when an u- s- a:: complaint against
7             an officer 'as been sustained. .h There's been forty,
8             documented cases of torture against, .h him and other
```

```
 9              police, detectives underneath him, .h and twenny uv
10              them have na::med him personally.=.hh Now, .h there's
11              been medical testimony, court testimony. .h u:m
12              ((swallow)).t ther:e's the Cook County deputy medical
13              examiner has, looked at, bur::ns on people's bodies,
14              .hhh and have said. yes. these are consistet- consistent
15              with bla:ck men's allegations against this man.=.h
16              Not only that, if the:y, were white suspects this would
17              n::ever, allowed- be ⌐allowed to con⌐tinue.
18   Audience:                     Lx - x - x -   LXXXXXXXXXXXX …
```

In response to Oprah's invitation, the contributor produces a lengthy utterance in which she constructs an argument in favor of a particular stance on the issue of police brutality. Note that the stance is not just stated, but her argument is supported by various types of evidence (principally, the deputy medical examiner's reports that she cites). Notice also that the audience's applause in line 18 is much more closely coordinated with the apparent completion of her argument than in the prior extract. The audience begins applauding once it is clear that the speaker is making the point that White suspects would not be subjected to this kind of treatment. She repairs the way this sentence is articulated twice, resulting in some overlap in the onset of applause; but despite that the applause is coordinated to begin in earnest halfway through the last word of the sentence, "con//tinue."

Throughout my data, this is the most characteristic form that opinion presentations take: relatively extended, multiunit turns, which are designed both to argue in favor of a particular stance and to provide some form of evidence or justification in support of that stance. In sequential terms, these extended turns exhibit a greater degree of coordination between the apparent conclusion of the turn and the onset of its response than do the shorter variants found in extracts (1) and (2). In the following, I argue that this has to do with the overall rhetorical structures that speakers utilize in order to produce structurally complete arguments.

Opinion presentations can be described as variants of what Schiffrin (1985) called "rhetorical arguments." Schiffrin studied everyday arguments and distinguished between shorter turns produced in interactive exchanges and those produced in more extended occupancy of the floor. The latter, rhetorical arguments, she described as discourses in which "a speaker presents an intact monologue supporting a disputable position"

(p. 37). In Schiffrin's account, rhetorical arguments are characterized, among other things, by the fact that they are produced using a combination of "descriptive" and "evaluative" talk. This distinction is not as straight-forward as it sounds, especially in the light of Pomerantz's (1984) claim that when speakers engage in descriptive talk of any kind (e.g., describing what is, what was, what happened, etc.), they unavoidably display in the details of the description an evaluative stance towards the description's truthfulness or accuracy. For instance, descriptions can be offered as true accounts of "the facts," or they can incorporate elements designed to display a degree of skepticism on the speaker's part. Another possibility is that the speaker may offer a "mere reporter's" account designed to present the information only "as known" to him or her. In short, there is an implicit evaluative element built into descriptive talk of any sort.

The point about rhetorical arguments, however, is that speakers articulate an evaluative stance on an issue explicitly, notwithstanding the stance implicit in their accompanying descriptions. One thing Schiffrin shows is that the evaluative components produced by speakers occupy distinctive spaces within the turn. For instance, one feature of the design of rhetorical arguments is that evaluative components regularly get placed at the boundaries of the argument-making turn.

The following extract, from Schiffrin's (1985) paper, illustrates this.

(4) [Schiffrin, 1985, p. 38]

1	Debbie:	And a lot of people believe that whatever's gonna
2		happen is gonna happen.
3	Irene:	I believe in that.
4	Debbie:	Whatever's gonna happen is gonna ⌐happen.
5	Irene:	└Yeh. I believe,
6		y'know it's fate. It really is. Because eh my husband
7		has a brother, that was killed in an automobile
8		accident, and at the same time there was another
9		fellow, in there, that walked away with not even a
10		<u>scratch</u> on him. And eh I really feel- I don't feel y'can
11		<u>push</u> fate and I think a lot of people <u>do</u>. But I feel
12		that you were put here for so many, years or whatever
13		the case is, and that's how it was meant to be. Because
14		like when we got married, we were supposed to get
15		married uh: like about five months later. My husband
16		got a notice tuh go into the service and we moved it

```
17                up. A:nd my father died the week, after we got married.
18                While we were on our honeymoon. And I just felt, that
19                move was meant to be, because if not, he wouldn't have
20                been there.
21   Debbie:     Yeh ⌈some⌉times-
22   Irene:          ⌊ So ⌋
23   Irene:      Eh y'know it just s-seems that that's how things work.
```

Here, beginning in line 5, Irene produces an extended turn in which she takes up and defends a position on the question of "fate." We can readily distinguish between the descriptive and evaluative components of this turn. The turn begins with an evaluative statement of belief: "I believe, y'know, it's fate" (lines 5–6). This evaluative component is followed (line 7 ff) by a passage of descriptive talk designed as a justification for Irene's position—and marked as such through the use of a subordinating conjunction, *because*. In this justification Irene uses a particular technique for providing reasoned grounds for a position (one that is also used with some frequency in talk radio and talk TV shows): She describes a relevant personal experience. Other position components (e.g., lines 11–13) and justifications (e.g., lines 13–20) are provided in the course of the turn. However, a third point to note is the way in which the argument is brought to a completion in lines 22–23, through the use of a summarizing component, or coda, marked as such by the sentence initial *So*—suggestive of the formulation of an upshot. In this coda, Irene encapsulates and reemphasizes the point that she has argued for in the evaluative phrase (line 23), "it just s-seems that that's how things work."

Thus, having (a) taken up a position, Irene displays a concern (b) to provide justifications for that position, and having done that, (c) to round off her argument with a summary statement of her position. In relation to this last point, two additional things can be noted. First, the coda is produced in overlap with Debbie's utterance "Yeh sometimes-" (line 21). Although it is possible that Irene, who comes in with "So" on the completion of Debbie's "Yeh," may have been continuing her turn by reference to the latter as a freestanding receipt object, nonetheless the fact that she actually goes on to hold the floor beyond Debbie's next item, "sometimes-," is indicative of a concern on her part to get this coda component done. Second, Irene's production of the coda, inasmuch as it rounds off the argument, can be seen as a means by which she signals the actual completion of the argument, and so indicates that she is relinquishing the floor after what has, in ordinary conversational terms, been an extended occupancy of it.

Thus, the format of the rhetorical argument in extract (4) can be described in terms of a three-stage model. In the first stage, the speaker "situates" herself in relation to an issue: A stance of some sort is taken up or adumbrated. In the second stage, a "case" is made for that stance: Some kind of justification or account is articulated. In the third stage, an evaluative coda formulates or recapitulates the "point" of the argument. This format, with the placing of evaluative components at the boundaries of the turn (beginning and end), can be a means by which the speaker not only constructs, but interactionally displays the construction of, a completed argument in favor of a position.

I have outlined this model using data drawn from a broadly conversational setting (in fact, the extract derives from informal sociolinguistic interviews carried out by Schiffrin, 1985). However, the same model can be used to account for the ways in which speakers on talk radio and talk TV shows construct their opinion presentations. Looking at the following extracts drawn from the talk radio data, we find that speakers use essentially the same format as Irene in extract (4) in order to present, defend, and mark the completion of their opinion presentations.

(5) [Talk Radio]

```
 1  Host:    Kath calling from Clapham now good morning.
 2  Caller:  Good morning Brian. Erm: I (li-) I also agree that thee
 3           .hh telethons a:re a form of psychological blackmail
 4           no:w. (.) .hhh Be:cause the majority of people I think
 5           do know that charities exist, .hh we all have our own
 6           charities that we contribute to:, (.) .h we do not have
 7           open ended pockets where we can keep on doing this.
 8           .hh And to sa:y because you have a credit car::d, .hh
 9           you just salve your conscience by paying- sending
10           in your number:, .phh I'm sorry but I: think that's
11           making people, (.) appear very erm (.) la:zy.=
12  Host:    =Well it's certainly not blackmail,
```

We see here that the caller produces a turn in which she first situates her stance by taking up a position in agreement with an earlier caller to the show (lines 2–4). She then makes a case for her stance (line 4 ff), offering a justificatory account—again, marked as such through the use of a conjunction, "Because . . ." (line 4). Finally, she produces an evaluative coda to mark the completion of the argument, employing what Heritage and Greatbatch (1986) described as a canonical format for position-taking: *I think + [Assessment]*; "I'm sorry but I: think that's making people, (.) appear very erm (.) la:zy."

Extract (6) shows a slightly different use of the same basic design format.

```
(6) [Talk Radio]
 1  Host:    It's Ka:y next from: Islington:, good morning.
 2  Caller:  Yes guh morning. Um:: (.) I: want to talk about thee-
 3           thee report on LBC this morning about Diana's visi:t
 4           to::, America:? h⌈.hh
 5  Host:                     ⌊The Princess of Wa:les.
 6           (.)
 7  Caller:  Princess of Wa:les, yah. .hh E::r th- her stay in a
 8           thou:sand pou:nds a night hotel plus V.A.T::, an' on
 9           her schedule she's visiting a home- p- place for the
10           homeless. .hhh A:nd there's going to be a ba::ll, .hh
11           where they're uh- the Americans are clamoring for
12           tickets at a thou:sand pounds a ni- er th- a thou:sand
13           pounds each, ⌈I:        th⌐ink it's obsce:ne.
14  Host:                ⌊Mm hm,⌡
15  Host:    .pt Which:, part is obsce:ne.
```

Instead of beginning her opinion presentation by stating a position, the caller here uses a different kind of situating component—a preface: "I: want to talk about thee- thee report on LBC this morning about Diana's visi:t to::, America:?." An account of circumstances surrounding the visit is then produced, in a way that will support her eventual statement of a position (e.g., by implying hypocrisy on the part of the Princess and others through a juxtaposition of expensive hotels and tickets for a ball with the problem of homelessness). Finally, the caller explicitly states the position she has been leading up to in the evaluative summary (again using the *I think + [Assessment]* format): "I: think it's obsce:ne."

The opinion presentation in this extract manifests a *progressional* dynamic, in contrast to the more *recursive* dynamic exhibited in extracts (4) and (5). In the *progressional pattern,* an opinion presentation goes from a relatively neutral situating component, through an account evi-

Argument Functions	Component Types	
	Recursive	**Progressional**
Part 1 Situating the argument	Position statement	Preface
Part 2 Making the case	Accounts & Justification	Accounts & Justification
Part 3 Rounding off the argument	Recapitulation	Position statement

FIGURE 1   A basic design format for opinion presentations.

dently designed to lead up to an evaluative conclusion, to a final assertion of that evaluation. In the *recursive pattern,* by contrast, a position is stated at the beginning, followed by a justificatory or supporting account, then the coda is used to recapitulate the initial position. In both variants, the point is that the three stages provide a sense of achieved completeness to an extended, argument-making turn.

Space prevents the presentation of further sets of examples; however, the basic format and its two main variants are summarized schematically in Figure 1, in which the three argument functions I have mentioned are matched with their associated basic discourse components.

It is important to note that there is a difference between what I have called the *achieved completeness* of the turn, in which this three-stage model is implicated, and its recognizable completeness.[5] I do not claim that this format generates arguments whose structural completion is necessarily observably oriented to by an interlocutor. Two types of evidence illustrate that arguments may be built to be complete without the necessity of being recognized as complete.

First, as extract (4) showed, it is possible for interlocutors to begin a response prior to what I have described as the structural completion points in an argument-making turn. Recall in that extract, as the recipient of the argument began talking, the first speaker displayed that she had not finished by carrying on, in overlap, to produce a coda, thus conforming to the recursive format described earlier:

(4) [Schiffrin, 1985, p. 38] *(Detail)*

```
18                    . . . And I just felt, that
19                    move was meant to be, because if not, he wouldn't have
20                    been there.
21    Debbie:    Yeh ⌈some⌉times-
22    Irene:          ⌊ So ⌋
23    Irene:    Eh y'know it just s-seems that that's how things work.
```

Second, there are instances in which even though the interlocutor does not produce a turn following a structural completion point, the speaker stops there, resulting in a gap. The following extract is a particularly clear example:

(7) [Talk Radio]

((The caller is reacting to a news story about poor people in Turkey being paid cash for their healthy bodily organs, which then Prime Minister Margaret Thatcher had described as "repugnant."))

```
 1   Host:      Maggie, .h Earls Court.
 2   Caller:    Oh hello yes I want to talk about the same subject. E::r
 3              what I'd like to say is, (1.0) e:r Margaret Thatcher
 4              doesn't mind people .hh paying surgeons to perform
 5              thee operation, .hh she doesn't mind people with more
 6              money jumping the queu:e, .hh again paying their money,
 7              .hh it seems to me what she finds repugnant, .hh is poor
 8              people getting money from the rich. .hh Which of course
 9              is completely against her policy.
10        →    (1.4)
11   Host:      We:ll I mean, .h that's not actually what she said.
```

Having presented her argument and taken up her position, the caller appears in line 11 to hand over the floor to the host, indicating that she considers that she has presented an argument that is complete enough to be understood and, perhaps, to warrant a response, although none is forthcoming until after a 1.4-sec silence (line 10).

Yet in the great majority of cases, structural completion points are indeed oriented to as such by the recipient, in the sense that they are used as a cue to start a response to the opinion presentation. One major reason for this is that completion markers take typical rhetorical forms, by means of which speakers bring their argument to a conclusion on a suitably tendentious note: a note that summarizes or emphatically evaluates the case being argued for. I refer to these rhetorical forms as *summative assessments*.

In everyday conversation, a characteristic way that speakers have of signaling a move towards the closure of an extended turn such as one in which a story has been told, a complaint put, or an argument forwarded, is to shift from description to the assessment of events (on stories, see Jefferson, 1978; Labov & Waletsky, 1967; on complaints, Drew & Holt, 1988; on arguments, Schiffrin, 1985; on strategy in political speeches,

Heritage & Greatbatch, 1986; and on assessments in general, Goodwin & Goodwin, 1990). For example, in the following extract, Hyla has been recounting the plot of a movie to her friend Nancy:

(8) [HG:II]

```
1   Hyla:        A:n then they go tuh this country club fer a party
2                an'the gu:y .hh u::m (0.2) an' they kick him out
3                becuz they find out he's Jewi:sh, .hh an' it's jus'
4        →       r:ril ly     s:::sa::d,
5   Nancy:            God that sounds  so goo::d?
```

Here, Hyla's "an' it's jus' r:rilly s:::sa::d" (lines 3–4) marks the point at which she shifts from descriptively recounting the story line to actively evaluating the movie. The assessment has a summative character that in this case seems to stem from the words "an' it's jus'," which mark the evaluation as a kind of rounding up (as we will see, a similar formulation is one of the typical summative assessments used in my data also). Nancy displays her own orientation to the completion-marking properties of the assessment by using it as the cue to start her response to Hyla's account of the movie.

In the talk radio data, various types of summative assessments are routinely used by callers. I have already noted that one of the most characteristic of these devices is *I think + [Assessment]*, which is similar to the device that Heritage and Greatbatch (1986), in their study of audience management devices in political speeches, referred to as "position-taking." In a second major class of completion markers, callers produce sentences incorporating "intensity" components, through which the egregiousness of the circumstances or events they are describing is emphasized:

(9) [Talk Radio]

```
1   Caller:   When you look at e:r the childcare facilities in this
2             country, .hh we're very very lo:w, (.) e- on the league
3             table in Europe of (.) yihknow if you try tuh get
4             a child into a nursery it's very difficult in this
5             country. .hh An' in fa:ct it's getting wor:se.
6   Host:     What's that got tuh do with it.
```

(10) [Talk Radio]

((Regarding a forthcoming increase in the state pension, following a recent reduction))

```
1   Caller:   Now, u-everythink is going up, an' buh the time they
2             give i' us back, .hh half the old age pensioners uh
3             be dead. (.)with the co:ld, (0.7) an:d an:d er, short
4             of food.
5   Host:     That's a little bit of an exaggeration . . .
```

(11) [Talk Radio]

((Regarding a TV program about the death of a suspect in police custody))

```
 1   Caller:   And uh they mentioned i- s-s- that 'e attended Sundee
 2             School. (.) Tha' 'ee wuz in the Boy:s Brigade. .h Thut 'e
 3             sang in a church choir. (.) .hhh And e:r th- (.) they
 4             didn' address the actual .p suh much the actual events
 5             or what led up to 'em or how many- people wen' intuh
 6             the shop with 'im whether the man wuz intimidated
 7             whether 'e tried to es:cape. .hhh And e- i'wuz just an
 8             a:nti police- (.) it was a police bashin' exercise
 9            ⎡(far as I-)
10   Host:    ⎣Well maybe- maybe it wa::s but I mean from what you've
11             told me: I must admit I would be a bit erm, .hhh tuh
12             say the least shocked by::, somebody being kill:ed under
13             those circumstances,
```

In each of these cases, callers produce summative assessments that emphasize just how complainable their complainable matters are. In extract (9), things are not just bad, but "in fa:ct it's getting wor:se"; in (10), a proposed pensions increase is not only paltry, but by the time it comes into effect "half the old age pensioners uh be dead"; and in (11), a TV program was not merely biased, it was a "police bashin' exercise."

In regard to the latter instance, it is noticeable that the caller in fact abandons what appears to be his first attempt to produce a completion component, "i' wuz just an a:nti police-" (note the similarities with "it's jus' r:rilly s:::sa::d" in extract [8]), in favor of an idiomatic (or figurative) version of the same sentiment: "it was a police bashin' exercise." In a study of idiomatic expressions in conversation, Drew and Holt (1988) found that one sequential location in which such expressions are routinely used is at the termination of a complaint. In particular, they suggested that idiomatic expressions may be used to "invite" the response of an uncooperative recipient by summarizing the complaint in a format sufficiently general to enable even a noncommittal affiliation (e.g., one phrased in similarly idiomatic terms). In this respect, idiomatic summations (such as "it was a police bashin' exercise") may serve as one member of a generic class of response-inviting formulations along with summations of the form *it was just [X]* and position-taking statements of the form *I think + [Assessment]*.

A further class of completion markers used by callers consists of sentences built as summative assessments incorporating phrases such as *of course* or *as you can imagine*. These formulations invite the recipient to see the "obviousness" or "reasonableness" of the speaker's conclusion.

(7) [Talk Radio] *(Detail)*

7		.hh it seems to me what she finds repugnant, .hh is poor
8		people getting money from the rich. .hh Which of course
9		is completely against her policy.
10		(1.4)
11	Host:	We:ll I mean, .h that's not actually what she said.

(12) [Talk Radio]

((Regarding people who object to the apartheid regime then in force in South Africa))

1	Caller:	But you see, when you a:sk them the question, would
2		they like- democracy:, erm- (.) universal franchi:se
3		one ma:n one vote, tomorrow, (.) ° .hhh° (0.2) they
4		a:ll seem to shift on their feet they're not su:re.
5		.hhh Because of course u-j-den:d up in chaos
6		y'cou⌐ldn' do=it y'd aff t'ave a⌐
7	Host:	└Well n-ay a- v- d- a:sk m-┘=
8	Caller:	=tra:nsiti⌐onal period, ┐
9	Host:	└Ask m- Ask m e: that question and see
10		what happen:s.

(13) [Talk Radio]

((Regarding dogs fouling public walkways))

1	Caller:	An' when I remonstrated with the lady, .h she told me
2		thut her dog ud got tuh do its bizniss somewhe:re, it

```
  3                  might as well be the:re.
  4    Host:        M:⌐m:,
  5    Caller:        └.phhh (.) A-::s you can imagine I: wuz absolutely:=
  6                 =livi⌐d(h),
  7    Host:               └We:ll did you- did yih then ek- explain that you
  8                  un:derstood that, yih know dogs have the call of nature
  9                  just as er as people do:: an' they do:n't have the same
 10                  kind uv contro:l, ((so therefore it's the owner's
 11                  responsibility))
```

There is a sense in which these kinds of formulations seek to implicate the respondent in the conclusion reached by the caller. What is noticeable, however, is that what they receive are expressly disaffiliative responses. In extract (7), the host disaffiliates by disagreeing with the caller's account of what Margaret Thatcher "said." In extract (12), the host disaffiliates with the caller's criticism of opponents of the apartheid regime in South Africa—that they "shift on their feet" when asked if they want to see the regime dismantled immediately—by instructing the caller to "ask me: that question and see what happen:s," thereby indicating that he is not going to shift on his feet. Finally, in extract (13), the caller has described her emotive reaction to the dog owner at the center of the complaint in the phrase "A-::s you can imagine I wuz absolutely: =livid(h)." The host disaffiliates by proposing that she make a coolly rational response to the woman by explaining that she understands the natural needs of dogs: In other words, he proposes a course of action on her part that is patently not the course of action she would have undertaken in the state of mind she has described.

In the talk radio data, then, there are numerous systematic ways that callers have of bringing home the point of their opinion presentations. Typically, these summative assessments express or encapsulate a contentious stance on the caller's part. On some occasions, the stance is expressed in such a way that the host is invited to see it as a reasonable conclusion; but on most occasions that is not the case. However, it is clear that, at least in the data at hand, hosts routinely treat callers' summative assessments as the cue to enter a disaffiliative or disputatious response, regardless of the way the evaluation appears to have been interactionally designed. This has to do with the confrontational nature of much talk radio interaction (Hutchby, 1996). The point to be emphasized for my purposes is that the devices described earlier all function effectively as oriented-to markers of completion in opinion presentations.

ACHIEVING COMPLETION AND
MANAGING APPLAUSE

Turning now to the Oprah Winfrey data, I expand on these remarks to look at how lay contributors in this different setting use rhetorical strategies, within the basic three-stage framework for opinion presentations, to display to the audience, and not just the host, when it might be timely to begin a response (i.e., to applaud). Two ways in which recipients may respond to opinion presentations are by affiliating or disaffiliating with the stance taken. On talk radio, the most typical reaction of the host to a caller's opinion is to challenge, dispute, be skeptical about, or otherwise disaffiliate from the stance that has been expressed (see Hutchby, 1992a, 1992b, 1996). In the talk TV materials, the host (or other recipients) may similarly offer challenges to or express skepticism about speakers' contributions; however, one feature of televised audience participation shows is that a large-scale audience is present, unlike on talk radio. In the data discussed here, the audience tends to affiliate with opinion presentations from lay speakers (but not, interestingly, those of experts) by applauding.

Responses produced by single speakers and those produced by a crowd differ not just in their properties (e.g., one takes the form of words whereas the other is nonlexical), but also in their sequential implications. That is, in these settings, applause seems to be more boundary marking than single speaker reactions tend to be. Indeed, throughout the Oprah Winfrey data, audience applause is followed not by the applauded speaker taking the floor again, but by Oprah introducing a next speaker (who may or may not be invited to address the point raised by the prior contributor) or even a next segment of the show. By contrast, when responses come from single speakers, in either setting, this usually results in an exchange of turns between the initial speaker and the respondent.

The upshot of this is that speakers are likely to know that audience applause will mark the end of their access to the floor, as the host moves on to a next speaker. It therefore becomes important that applause occurs at the right place, otherwise, again, the point may never be made in the desired way. As the following extracts show, speakers in this setting—who are by no means as polished or coached in public speaking as politicians, for example—in fact are capable of strategically managing the occurrence of applause as effectively, and by means of essentially similar rhetorical devices, as Atkinson (1984) found professional politicians and other public speakers do.

Returning to extract (3), the first thing to notice is that this speaker builds her opinion presentation using the three-stage format described earlier:

(3) [*Oprah Winfrey Show*]

```
 1  Oprah:    You say what ma'am?
 2  Woman:    I say that thee, u:h report that's sitting on
 3            Superintendent Martin's desk which is, he's thee: head
 4            of thee oaf- Officer Professional Standards which is the
 5            internal police investigative body, .hh o:nly goe:s, .h
 6            tuh his desk, .h when an u- s- a:: complaint against
 7            an officer 'as been sustained. .h There's been forty,
 8            documented cases of torture against, .h him and other
 9            police, detectives underneath him, .h and twenny uv
10            them have na::med him personally.=.hh Now, .h there's
11            been medical testimony, court testimony. .h u:m
12            ((swallow)).t ther:e's the Cook County deputy medical
13            examiner has, looked at, bur::ns on people's bodies,
14            .hhh and have said. yes. these are consistet- consistent
15            with black men's allegations against this man ꞊ h
16            Not only that, if the:y, were white suspects this would
17            n::ever, allowed- be ⌐allowed to con⌐tinue.
18  Audience:              ⌊x - x - x -  ⌊XXXXXXXXXXXX ...
```

The turn is opened with a position statement (lines 2–8), in which the caller asserts that complaints only go to the internal investigative body of the police when they are actually sustained. This sets up an expectation that the speaker knows of other complaints that have not been sustained, and so are not known about by the named officer, "Superintendent Martin." In a case-making section in lines 8–15, the speaker justifies her stance by citing evidence of "forty documented cases of torture" and the deputy medical examiner's assertion that medical evidence is consistent with the allegations of Black victims. Finally, in lines 16–17, a summative assessment rounds off the argument: "if the:y were white suspects this would n::ever . . . be allowed to continue."

Immediately following this summative assessment (indeed, in slight overlap with its completion) there is enthusiastic applause from the audience. I noted in the previous section that summations on talk radio take certain regular forms. The common property of these kinds of components is that they serve to emphasize the fact that a point is currently being made; in this sense, they are members of the class of what Heritage and Greatbatch (1986) referred to as position-taking devices. In their study, Heritage and Greatbatch found this to be "the most effective single rhetorical format" (p. 131) associated with audience applause. In this device

> The speaker first describes a state of affairs towards which he or she could be expected to take a strongly evaluative stance. . . . At the end of it, the speaker overtly and unequivocally praises or condemns the state of affairs described. (p. 131)

The speaker's final sentence in extract (3), "if the:y were white suspects this would n::ever . . . be allowed to continue," is thus, of course, a position-taking device. However it also possesses other properties that are related to the general features of rhetorical devices discussed by Heritage and Greatbatch (1986), and which play an important role in enabling the audience successfully to coordinate its applause with the payoff to the speaker's opinion presentation. Following Atkinson (1984), Heritage and Greatbatch (1986) argued that rhetorical devices that are effective in generating applause tend to work because of two properties:

> (a) [they] *emphasize* and thus highlight their contents against a surrounding background of speech materials and (b) [they] *project a clear completion point* for the message in question. Atkinson proposes that these two requirements are satisfied by certain conventionalized rhetorical formats—in particular, the contrast (or antithesis) and the three-part list. (p. 116)

For instance, a contrastive pair succeeds in generating applause because the audience can judge, during the unfolding of what is recognizably the second part of a contrast, what it will take for the contrast to be completed and so coordinate its response with that completion. The three-part list works because, as Jefferson (1990) has shown, there is a conventionalized expectation, in everyday interaction as well as oratory, that lists can be treated as complete after three items. Indeed, Jefferson discussed the phenomenon of the "generalized list completer," phrases such as *and everything, or something, and so on,* which speakers routinely append to lists containing two items in order to turn them into three-part lists. Given this conventional property of lists in conversation, audiences can project that if a list is being constructed by the speaker, it is likely to be complete after the third item, at which point applause can be coordinated. (We see the effectiveness of three-part lists in extract [14] following.)

With these comments in mind, it is clear that although the speaker's final sentence in extract (3) is neither a three-part list nor a contrastive pair, it nonetheless has similar projective properties. Principally, the utterance is constructed as a "compound unit" (Lerner, 1987) of the *if [X] then [Y]* type. Lerner showed such compound units are systematically vulnerable to collaborative completion in everyday conversation, precisely because a recipient of the first part can project what it will take to complete the construction. As we see, the audience in extract (3) is able to use that format to project the place at which the speaker's summation will be complete, and indeed begins applauding slightly in overlap with its completion.

Let us look at another extract from the Oprah Winfrey data. Note that in this extract, contrary to almost all the others discussed so far, the speaker's opinion presentation does not take the form of an uninterrupted rhetorical argument, but is interspersed with questions and challenges from the host. We can observe how these interjections have specific consequences for the rhetorical design of the argument, but also how they furnish additional evidence for the oriented-to effectiveness of the formats and devices I have described.

(14) [*Oprah Winfrey Show*]

```
 1   Oprah:     Okay=Whaddayou say sir?
 2   Man:       .thhh It's not just a question uv individual cops being
 3              racist er no:t. .hh The police department as itse:lf,
 4              (.) is a racist institution. (0.5) .hhh An' I'll give
 5              y'en exa:mple.=In December uv this yea:r, (0.5) the
 6              London office uv A:mnesty International issued the
 7              first time ever. (.) .hh an accusation against the Sh-
 8              uh police department in the U.S., (.) .hh fuh using
 9              torture against suspects=right here the Chicago Police
10              Department.=
11   ( ):       =ku:⌈h  huh⌉
12   Oprah:         ⌊Mmhm.⌋ =
13   Man:       =has been doing this since nineteen sevenny two:.
14   Oprah:     .pt Has been doing wha:t.
15   Man:       Using electro sho::ck, (0.4) bur:ns, (0.2) suffocation,
16              .hhh an' threatened execution on black prisoners=a:ll
17              black prisoners it's ⌈a racist-
18   Oprah:                          ⌊How do you know that.
19              (0.3)
```

```
20   Man:        .hhh Cuz there are a:ffadavits, OPS complaints, (0.8)
21               .thh testimo:ny an' depositions. (.) in civil cases going
22               back.=The Chicago Police Department has promoted him
23               from the ra:nks, .hhh until today he's one o' the highest
24               ranking o:fficers in the Chicago Police Department. .hhh
25               That sends a message tuh every cop in thuh department
26               that the way tuh get ahead in Chicago, .hh is to be
27               racist, (.) violent, (.) an' even to use torture. .h=
28   Audience:   =x⌈x-XXXXXXXXXXXXXX ⌈XXXXXXXXXXXXXXXXXXX . . .
29   Audience:      ⌊WOOO⌈OOOOOO!          ⌊
30   Audience:           ⌊WOOOoo!    ⌊Woo⌈hoo!
31   Audience:                            ⌊WOOO!
```

Examining how the speaker constructs his argument in the context of the interjections from Oprah Winfrey, in lines 14 ("Has been doing wha:t") and 18 ("How do you know that"), we see how different rhetorical devices can be used in the same opinion presentation to make successive attempts to present a structurally complete argument.

Oprah's two interjections are of different types. The first, in line 14, appears to be designed to clarify or disambiguate the anaphora in the speaker's immediately prior description, "has been doing this since nineteen sevenny two:."[6] The interactional significance of Oprah's "Has been doing wha:t" is that it provides the speaker with the opportunity to produce a list of the alleged unlawful practices used by the police department on "black prisoners=a:ll black prisoners." This formulation in turn leads into what strongly appears to be a summative assessment (line 17: "it's a racist-") that, recalling our discussion of the recursive format for opinion presentations, would be a recapitulation of the position statement he began with (i.e., lines 3–4: "the police department as itsel:f, (.) is a racist institution").

At this point, then, the speaker has constructed a virtually complete argument in the recursive format, which has not been obstructed but actually assisted by Oprah's interjection. However, Oprah's next interjection serves to interrupt what appears to be an attempt at a summation, and the speaker cuts off before finishing. Oprah's overlap comes slightly too early (i.e., after "it's" in "it's a racist-") to enable us to suggest that she herself recognizes that the speaker is about to move to a summative assessment, and thus interrupts before the audience can applaud. Yet the talk produced in overlap by the speaker indicates that this may well be what he was intending at that point, which makes Oprah's intervention timely from her perspective, since otherwise her question is likely to have been competing with audience applause.

It is noticeable that Oprah's interruption in line 21 takes the form of a challenge: "How do you know that." This turn does not merely seek to clarify a term of reference, but requires the caller to go on to provide further information in support of his stance. Whether Oprah does this supportively, aiming to strengthen the speaker's stance by requiring further justifications, or critically, is unclear. However, the point is that the speaker now has to redesign the completion of his argument.

This turns out to provide further evidence that lay speakers in this setting can rely on the same kinds of rhetorical strategies for managing audience applause as professional orators. After providing further justificatory components in lines 20–24, the speaker moves again to a completion, this time using an extremely well-crafted three-part list:

> That sends a message tuh every cop in thuh
> department that the way tuh get ahead in Chicago,
> .hh is to be racist,
> (.) violent,
> (.) an' even to use torture.

As in the data discussed by Atkinson (1984), this list succeeds in generating a highly coordinated response from the audience, not only by virtue of the conventionalized nature of lists of three, but also through the speaker's vocal comportment:[7] The first two items in the list are produced with slightly rising intonation, and a tiny gap is left after each part; the final part is produced with a falling intonation, thereby underlining the fact that the list is indeed now completed.

CONCLUSION

This article has two main aims: to show that lay speakers in audience participation TV and radio debates use a common rhetorical format in opinion presentations that enables them to design their arguments so as to be structurally complete and to explore some of the implications of that format for the management of responses to opinion presentations. I showed that the three-stage model outlined in Figure 1 represents a systematic format that enables speakers to construct two types of argument: a recursive type and a progressive type. Within these frameworks, speakers in the settings of talk radio, which involves person-to-person interaction with the host, and talk TV, which can additionally involve interaction with a large-scale copresent audience, are able to construct arguments on a variety of topics, and recipients of those utterances are, for the most part, able to coordinate appropriately timed responses to the argument.

We have also seen how lay speakers, who are not coached in public speaking in the same way as professional politicians, actually use essentially similar rhetorical devices to manage the applause of audiences to their points. Thus, although certain aspects of rhetoric may be written into the speeches that politicians give, there is strong evidence that persons can "intuitively" use such devices in order to signal to an audience that they are coming to the completion of an extended, argument-making turn. Although it is clear that speakers in settings such as the *Oprah Winfrey Show* are often very well prepared (the speaker in extract [14] in fact brought the Amnesty International report he refers to with him and brandishes it during his speech), it is equally clear that they are not reading from a script or from "idiot" boards as many politicians are known to do. Similarly, though there may possibly be elements of their utterances that they have memorized, the analysis of extract (14) indicates that even when one attempt to rhetorically round off an opinion presentation does not work, the speaker is able to produce a second, and in this case better designed, rhetorical completion.

One final point concerns the relation between this analysis and that of Atkinson (1984) and Heritage and Greatbatch (1986). A significant difference between the nature of rhetoric and response in political platform speeches and on talk radio and talk TV is that in the former setting the speaker will be seeking numerous bursts of applause in the course of a much longer speech. On talk radio and talk TV, however, the lay contributor typically can be assured of only one opportunity to make their point (others may occur, but only one is actually ensured). There are thus important temporal constraints within which lay contributors must work. It is this, I suggest, that leads to the three-stage rhetorical format being so widely used in these settings. Given that contributors are given the space to make only one central point, there is considerable pressure on them to make it in the most economical, yet most effective, way they can. Designing arguments in which one's position is first adumbrated (or even stated), then provided with support and justification, then expressed in unequivocal terms, is both economical and effective in the task of having one's say within such constraints.

NOTES

1   The analysis presented here relies in part on observations I originally presented at the International Seminar on Broadcast Talk, Strathclyde University, Glasgow, Scotland, September 1992. Although a large proportion of the ideas contained in the current article postdate that presentation, many of the comments made by participants in the seminar have found their way, ultimately, into my analysis. I would therefore like to acknowledge the contributions of Deborah Cameron, Martin Montgomery, Paddy Scannell, Jenny Thomas, and Joanna Thornborrow. On the article as it appears here, Alan Firth and, especially, Robert Sanders made extremely useful comments. Needless to say, responsibility for any shortcomings is mine alone.

2   This corpus contains approximately 140 calls to the show, and three different hosts appear in the data. For a fuller analysis of this data corpus, see Hutchby (1996).

3   The Chicago Police Department was not, of course, directly involved in the Rodney King case, which was brought against the Los Angeles Police Department. However, the show in question was designed to discuss the question of the police more broadly, using Rodney King as a starting point.

4   This distinguishes the kind of show I am interested in from other forms of debate in which the audience is restricted to asking questions of panel members. In the British context, shows such as the British Broadcasting Corporation's *Any Questions* and *Question Time* fall into the latter category. By "debate show" in this article, I mean shows in which audience participants are invited and encouraged to express opinions in their own right.

5   I am grateful to Robert Sanders for impressing this point on me.

6   Recall that in extract (6) earlier, the talk radio host produced a similar clarifying turn in the midst of a caller's opinion presentation, there designed to establish that the "Diana" referred to by the caller was in fact "the Princess of Wales."

7   Atkinson also shows that bodily comportment is a significant factor; however, to show that in this case would require a more detailed analysis of gesture than is possible given current space limitations.

REFERENCES

Atkinson, J. M. (1984). *Our masters' voices: The language and body language of politics.* London: Methuen.

Drew, P., & Holt, E. (1988). Complainable matters: The use of idiomatic expressions in making complaints. *Social Problems, 35,* 398–417.

Goodwin, C., & Goodwin, M. H. (1990). Assessments and the construction of context. In A. Duranti & C. Goodwin (Eds.), *Rethinking context* (pp. 151–189). Cambridge, England: Cambridge University Press.

Heritage, J., & Greatbatch, D. (1986). Generating applause: A study of rhetoric and response at party political conferences. *American Journal of Sociology, 19,* 110–157.

Hutchby, I. (1992a). Confrontation talk: Aspects of 'interruption' in argument sequences on talk radio. *Text, 12,* 343–371.

Hutchby, I. (1992b). The pursuit of controversy: Routine scepticism in arguments on talk radio. *Sociology, 26,* 673–694.

Hutchby, I. (1996). *Confrontation talk: Arguments, asymmetries and power on talk radio.* Mahwah, NJ: Lawrence Erlbaum Associates, Inc.

Jefferson, G. (1978). Sequential aspects of storytelling in conversation. In J. Schenkein (Ed.), *Studies in the organization of conversational interaction* (pp. 219–248). New York: Academic.

Jefferson, G. (1990). List construction as a task and resource. In G. Psathas (Ed.), *Interaction competence* (pp. 63–92). Washington, DC: University Press of America.

Labov, W., & Waletsky, J. (1967). Narrative analysis: Oral versions of personal experience. In J. Helm (Ed.), *Essays on the verbal and visual arts* (pp. 12–44). Seattle: University of Washington Press.

Lerner, G. (1987, August). *On the syntax of sentences-in-progress.* Paper presented at the Eighth International Conference for Ethnomethodology and Conversation Analysis, Boston University, Boston, MA.

MacDonald, A. M. (Ed.). (1981). *Chambers Twentieth Century Dictionary.* Edinburgh: W. & R. Chambers Ltd.

Pomerantz, A. (1984). Giving a source or basis: The practice in conversation of telling 'how I know'. *Journal of Pragmatics, 8,* 607–625.

Schiffrin, D. (1985). Everyday argument: The organization of diversity in talk. In T. A. van Dijk (Ed.), *Handbook of discourse analysis, vol. 3* (pp. 35–46). London: Academic.

Thornborrow, J. (1997). Having their say: The function of stories in talk show discourse. *Text, 17,* 241–262.

Research on Language and Social Interaction, 32(3), 269–302
Copyright © 1999, Lawrence Erlbaum Associates, Inc.

Narrating the Game: Achieving and Coordinating Partisanship in Real Time

Alan D. Hansen
Department of Communication
University at Albany, SUNY

Two simultaneous real-time broadcasts of a college football game are analyzed to reveal how pairs of broadcasters, partisan to one of the teams involved, interactively coconstruct a partisan narrative of the play on the field. By praising home team players when they succeed and providing mitigating accounts of these players' failures, partisanship is constructed. Viewing the play-by-play and color commentary as account making, the analysis reveals that the partisan quality of praising, blaming, mitigating, and the like arises from how the action is accounted for. The analysis also reveals that turn-allocation conventions within each booth have consequences for coordination on the emerging partisan narrative.

As a genre of mass media discourse, sports broadcasting is highly structured and comprises two kinds of talk: *play-by-play,* a description of the ongoing action, and *color commentary,* a narrative composed of

---

This article is a revision of a paper presented at the Sixth International Conference on Narrative, Lexington, KY, November 1997.

I thank the members of the Research Proseminar of the University at Albany Communication Department for their helpful comments over the course of this project. I also thank Robert Sanders for his guidance during the entire project and editorial advice in its later stages and the anonymous reviewers for their helpful suggestions for revision. Regardless of the abundant support I received on this project, I of course am solely responsible for its weaknesses.

Correspondence concerning this article should be sent to Alan D. Hansen, Department of Communication, BA 119, University at Albany, SUNY, 1400 Washington Avenue, Albany, NY 12222. E-mail: ah0019@cnsvax.albany.edu

background information and interpretation of the action. In cases in which there are two broadcasters, one commonly is responsible for the play-by-play and the other for the color commentary (Ferguson, 1983). Coordinating speaking turns to describe and evaluate the action, broadcasters produce a single emerging narrative account of the game. The narrative—about players, the quality of the team(s) or the game in progress, trends over the season or years, and so forth—is developed and sustained primarily in the color commentary, sometimes based on characterizations provided in the description of the unfolding action.[1]

Sports broadcasters construct a narrative, in real time, that is attuned to the expectations and collective agenda of their broadcast audience. This is true whether the broadcast is intended for a national, bipartisan audience, or whether the broadcast is intended for a regional, partisan audience. There has been some recognition that partisan narratives are shaped by broadcasters, and some attention to how this is done. For instance, this critique of partisan sports broadcasting illustrates how broadcasters might advance a partisan agenda in narrating the game:

> You can't listen to a game—be it baseball, football, basketball or hockey—nowadays without some shill invoking the loyal "we," complaining about the officiating against "us," alibiing for poor coaching or trumpeting a nice play by "our" team as the greatest of athletic feats. ... [A] hard hit by one of "our guys" equals a cheap shot by one of "their guys." (Wulf, 1993, p. 190)

In this study I analyze the way partisan narratives are coconstructed in broadcasts of the same game from two radio broadcast booths, each partisan to one of the teams involved. I show how the broadcasters in these two booths achieve a partisan narrative of the action. Here I consider partisanship as it is displayed through the broadcasters' way of formulating praise and criticism of the home team and its players, and of the opposing team and its players, in adhering to the partisan agenda of portraying the home team in a favorable light. This is congruent with Wulf's (1993) ideas about partisan narration and also Emmison's (1987, 1988). In analyzing interviews between broadcasters and participants following sports contests, Emmison (1987) found that partisan broadcasters congratulated "home team" players in victory by praising them, and produced "mitigating accounts" of the action to commiserate with home team players in defeat.

Emmison (1988) also found that the participants in the interviews often coordinated to produce partisan accounts of the action. In this study I consider how the coordination itself between the broadcasters may shape the partisan narrative. As noted earlier, the broadcasters' partisan agenda in narrating the game is to portray the home team and its players in a favorable light. However, the broadcast talk is driven by the facts of the external event (Kuiper, 1995) and the players may succeed or fail in a given play; accordingly, a genuine narrative—even if partisan—cannot avoid references to failures by home team players. Because the broadcasters' respective contributions to the partisan narrative must be consistent both with the event itself and with their own previous talk, their coordination in constructing a narrative of the action ultimately is consequential to what the narrative account ends up being.

Accordingly, I first show how the broadcasters formulate their talk to advance their partisan agenda—to portray the home team and its players in the best possible light. I then show different "interaction constraints" in the way the broadcasters in the two broadcast booths coordinated to narrate the game. Finally, I show the ways in which these interaction constraints are consequential to what the respective partisan narratives ended up being.

PARTISANSHIP IN SPORTS BROADCAST NARRATIVES

Agency and Accountability

The role of sports broadcasters is to describe the action on the field in real time and, when not rendering these descriptions, provide background commentary and interpretations of the action just occurring (Ferguson, 1983; Kuiper, 1995). Because players' efforts succeed or fail in the course of the game, the players—and their efforts—are subject to praise or criticism. In order to produce a partisan narrative, the broadcasters provide *accounts*—verbal responses to actions that merit some degree of praise or criticism (see Buttny, 1993). With these accounts, partisan broadcasters systematically portray the home team and its players in a positive light by praising them when successful and by providing mitigating accounts of the players' failures.

However, because players' actions are not isolated, the accounts provided by partisan broadcasters are complicated. Not only may the same player succeed at one moment and fail at the next, but descriptions of the action themselves have partisan implications and may need to be adjusted to align with the partisan narrative developed thus far. Thus, the description of the action in real time and interpretation of action just occurring involve accounts as well as modifications to previous accounts. In providing and modifying their narrative accounts, the broadcasters establish the basis for a player's accountability for a given action.

Agency is an important consideration in establishing accountability. Players cannot be held accountable—blameworthy or praiseworthy—unless they are characterized by the broadcasters as responsible, in some way, for their actions. Thus, in analyzing the construction of a partisan narrative, I give particular attention to the broadcasters' attributions of agency for plays and their outcome.

Excerpt (1) following shows how the broadcasters attribute agency to a home team player and orient to the partisan implications of this attribution. In this excerpt, the play-by-play broadcaster for Booth 1 (hereafter P_1) and the color broadcaster for Booth 1 (hereafter C_1) coordinate to describe and interpret the action: The quarterback (Hilde) for the Broncos (the home team for Booth 1) is tackled behind the line of scrimmage. This constitutes a negative outcome for the Broncos and a positive outcome for the Vandals (the opposing team for Booth 1).

(1) (Booth 1: home team = Broncos, opposing team = Vandals) [1:116–124]

1	P_1:	The Vandals, show <u>six</u> men on the uh line of
2		scrimmage,=in motion (4.2) is Richmond,=Hilde <u>keeps</u>
3		it, gets back to the line of scr<u>imm</u>age, no:, he loses
4		a couple a yards back to the <forty five>, as they
5		>got 'em with the< blitz that time.
6	C_1:	Well Tim Wilson was the first guy there and made Tony
7		cut back up and there were a >couple of other<, black
8		jerseys there.
9		(0.2)
10	C_1:	You know, you guess you could <u>c</u>all it a sack, but uh:,
11		(.) Tony bailed >out a there< real quick,=he saw a lot
12		of black jerseys and <u>bail</u>ed out.

The real-time description by P_1 (in lines 1–5) asserts the agency of the home team quarterback (Hilde), by stating Hilde "<u>keeps</u> it, gets back to the line of <u>scrimmage</u>" (lines 2–3). This description establishes Hilde as the one "doing" the action. As the action unfolds, P_1 (lines 3–4) revises his real-time description that Hilde has gotten back to the line of scrimmage, stating Hilde "loses a couple a yards." The negative consequence of this revision for the partisan narrative is that Hilde, described as the agent of the action, is now responsible for the loss of yardage. However, P_1 withdraws agency from Hilde and attaches it to the opposing team by offering a third version of his real-time description: "They [the opposing team] >got 'em [the home team] with the< blitz that time" (lines 4–5). This formulation identifies the opposing team as the agent of the action and the home team (and Hilde) as the party acted on; at the same time the description also avoids warranting praise to defensive players for the opposing team who were involved in the action, by referring to them en masse as an anonymous "they."

In the interpretive commentary that follows, the initial contribution by C_1 (lines 6–8) can be seen as an elaboration of the final formulation by P_1: C_1 identifies a player from the opposing team (Tim Wilson) as the agent of the action, and positions "our" quarterback (Tony Hilde) as the party acted on. Additionally, C_1 specifies the action imposed by the agent, stating Wilson "made Tony cut back up" (lines 6–7). However, this formulation now warrants praise of a player for the opposing team, and seems to undermine the broadcasters' partisan agenda to attribute agency to players in such a way as to portray the home team player in a favorable light. However, a self-initiated repair immediately follows. In his second interpretation of the action, C_1 finds a way to both award agency to the home team player for a praiseworthy action and withdraw agency from the opposing team player. By stating that Hilde "bailed >out a there< real quick" (line 11), C_1 characterizes Hilde's action of bailing out not as a passive reaction to the imposition of an outside agent, but as a proficient strategic maneuver. This account is notably different from the original version of the narrative, which was provided in real time.

The partisanship of the narrative produced in Booth 1 is amplified when it is contrasted with the way the same play was described and commented on in Booth 2. Note that the partisan aspect is reversed in this booth: Their home team is the defense, and the play constitutes a positive outcome for the Vandals (home team for Booth 2), and a negative outcome for the Broncos (opposing team for Booth 2).

(2) (Booth 2: home team = Vandals, opposing team = Broncos) [2:112–117]

1   P_2:   . . . and back to pass is Hilde,=rolls to the right
2   comes up=hit! (.) and dropped (.) for a loss (.) as

```
3        Wilson comes through for the sack.
4        (1.7)
5   P₂:  Tim Wilson had three big sacks last week, and that's
6        his <sixth sack> of the season (.) and Tim Wilson a
7        sophomore from Seattle nails 'im, for a loss of about
8        three or four ya:rds, (0.2) it's close to four yards back at the
9        forty six,=we'll call it second down and (.) oh:=thirteen and a half
10       to ↓go.
```

The play-by-play broadcaster for Booth 2 (hereafter P₂), in describing the action on the field, awards agency to the home team player (Wilson) by describing him as "com[ing] through for the sack" (line 3). This was elaborated in his subsequent commentary in which Wilson's record of making such plays was cited (lines 5–6). In addition, Wilson's action in this play was magnified in force in the interpretive commentary, described as "nail[ing]" Hilde (line 7). On the other hand, Hilde is consistently portrayed as a nonagent—a passive object of Wilson's actions.

The preceding excerpts illustrate how agency figures into the partisan narrative: The broadcasters construct and sustain a partisan narrative by magnifying the agency of home team players for praiseworthy actions and suppressing the agency of home team players for blameworthy actions. Similarly, the partisan narrative consists of denying the agency of opposing team players for their successes and identifying them as agents of blameworthy actions.

The broadcasters, however, are not restricted to characterizing only players as agents of the action on the field of play; third parties also are praiseworthy or blameworthy. Among the third parties eligible for praise and blame are coaches, spectators, and (perhaps most commonly) referees (see Emmison, 1988). Thus, in accounting for a failure by the home team and its players, the broadcasters may implicate a third party in order to portray the home team in a positive light.

The importance of agency in the partisan narrative shows that attributions of free choice constitute a necessary condition for accountability (Buttny, 1993). Thus, in constructing a partisan narrative, attributing agency is a prerequisite for allocating praise and blame. The excerpts earlier show how the broadcasters award agency, or deny agency, to the players. In Booth 1, excerpt (1), the broadcasters ultimately awarded agency to Hilde and denied it to Wilson. In Booth 2, excerpt (2), the reverse occurred: Wilson was consistently characterized as the agent and Hilde as a passive recipient of the action.

Mitigating and Intensifying Accountability

Constructing a partisan narrative is more complicated than simply awarding and denying agency and issuing praise and blame accordingly. Accountability for bringing about a result through one's action is not black and white but can be a matter of degree. In seeking evidence that the agent was responsible for the result of his or her actions, and should be praised or blamed, one has to assert first, that the agent was equipped with the resources and experience to control the result through his or her actions, and second, that the agent exhibited the effort and intentions needed to control the result through his or her actions (see Buttny, 1993, pp. 3–4). The former evidence that the agent was accountable for bringing about the result is weaker, more circumstantial, than the latter, making the agent less deserving of praise or blame. Hence, to call attention to a successful player's physical advantage and superior experience, not effort and intentions, would mitigate praise. Conversely, accountability can be denied by citing evidence that the agent did not exhibit the requisite effort or intentions or that the agent lacked the resources and experience needed. Hence, for broadcasters to call attention to an unsuccessful player's physical disadvantage and inexperience, or both, is to mitigate blame.

Similarly, because the players are perceived as having more control over their effort and intentions than they have over their ability and experience (see Buttny, 1993), to mitigate praise or intensify blame the broadcasters may portray the player as putting forth very little effort or as not having the necessary intentions. Similarly, to allocate praise or mitigate blame the broadcasters may characterize the player as putting forth maximum effort or as having the right intentions.

Consider excerpt (3) following, in which the broadcasters in Booth 1 call attention to the inexperience of a home team player in order to mitigate blame. In this excerpt, the home team's Jeff Davis is punting the ball to the opposition; the opposing team almost blocks the kick.

(3) (Booth 1: home team = Broncos, other team = Vandals) [1:169–182]

1	P₁:	Good snap from center, (.) the kick is almost blocked
2		(0.5) and goes out of bounds? no not yet it's picked
3		up at the: fiftee:n, and a broken ↑<tackle:> (.) and
4		down at the thirty yard line on a: nice punt return on
5		the far side of the field by Ted Seve:re.
6	C₁:	You know >I'll tell you- < Jeff Davis=we haven't said

```
 7        →     much about it, but he's gotta learn to get a little
 8               quicker.
 9               (.)
10   C₁:   →     He just takes his time like he's out there in
11               practice, somebody's gotta >whop'm on side the< head
12               and say ki:d, you see somebody comin off the side and=
13   P₁:           ⌈Kick! the ball⌉
14   C₁:         =⌊he's not block⌋ed (0.2) kick it.=Ya gotta move it
15               ya gotta get it goin.
16   P₁:   →     Just a freshman, (0.2) and Pokey said on Thursday
17               night's show that <he will learn> but ah (.) the
18               Broncos have had punts blocked in the last two weeks
19               (0.2) an:d, u::h, may have been a partial block in
20               the:re.
```

In his commentary, C_1 identifies Jeff Davis, the home team punter, as the agent of the action, and blames him for the near-blocked kick. C_1 criticizes Davis for being too slow (lines 7–8) and for approaching the kick "like he's out there in practice" (lines 10–11). This critique of the home team player seems to imply that Davis is careless and lazy, which undermines the broadcasters' partisan agenda to portray the home team and its players in a favorable light. However, analysis of the critique by C_1 also shows some evidence of mitigating the criticism by calling attention to Davis' inexperience: C_1 prefaces his critique by stating that Davis has "gotta learn" (line 7) and refers to Davis as "kid," which calls attention to and reinforces his inexperience (line 12). P_1 further mitigates the blame that C_1 placed on Davis also by calling attention to his inexperience (lines 16–17): He is "just a freshman" and "will learn."

In considering excerpt (3) preceding, the question remains: Given the partisan agenda of portraying the home team in a positive light, why would C_1 offer such a pointed critique of a home team player? One might offer excerpt (3) as counterevidence of the notion that these broadcasters have a partisan agenda at all. However, the work done by the broadcasters to mitigate the criticism—particularly the work by P_1—suggests that a partisan agenda is at work despite the criticism. Considering the alternatives available to the broadcasters—portraying the player as lazy, inept, apathetic, and so forth—a critique of the home team player on the basis of inexperience, which also emphasizes that the player will learn, clearly mitigates the blame. Thus, excerpt (3) illustrates the partisan broadcasters' challenge in providing unscripted commentary: The circumstances of the external event may make it difficult to advance the partisan agenda and thus compel the broadcasters to modify their accounts in order to produce a coherent partisan narrative.

A second, more powerful basis for attributing responsibility is the effort and intentions of a player. Thus, attributing responsibility for a result on the basis of manifest effort and intentions is a way to maximize praise of players for praiseworthy actions. Consider excerpt (4) following, from Booth 2. Here the Vandals (home team for Booth 2) succeed in completing a long pass to MacKenzie, the home team receiver. For the broadcasters in Booth 2 the play has a considerable favorable outcome, earning their team "a first down";[2] thus, they praise MacKenzie by awarding agency to him and maximize the praise by establishing a strong basis for agency.

(4) (Booth 2: home team = Vandals, other team = Broncos) [2:434–448]

1	P₂:	... back to pass has forever, goes for a streak (0.2)
2		going to MacKenzie down field it i:s (0.2) CAUGHT! BY
3		MACKENZIE. A GREAT CATCH BY MACKENZIE (.) AS IT WAS
4		DEFLECTED (.) by <Jason Pa:yne> as both of em went up
5		for it (.) down deep on the Boise State thirty four.
6	→	Give MacKenzie all of the credit for that one.
7		(.)
8	P₂:	Oh! what a gra:b. Talk about (.) <u>real real</u>
9		concentration on the ball, Dwight MacKenzie had it
10		there, (.) a forty seven yard pick up (.) first down
11		and ten for the Vandals (.) on the ↑ Bronco: thirty
12		fou:⌈r:.⌉
13	C₂:	⌊M⌋cKenzie wanted that one,=had his hand up all
14		the way down on the route said I- I'm gonna get this no
15		matter wha:t, went ↑up for it (.) an:d you talk about
16		w- the only thing in the wor:ld that, mattered to
17		Dwight MacKenzie was that <u>foot</u>ball no matter <u>who</u> was on
18		and he had it as he was falling down, Bob.
19	P₂:	Jason Payne was in good coverage (.) MacKenzie just out
20		fought 'im for it.

In describing the action in real time, P_2 identifies MacKenzie, the home team receiver of the pass, as the agent of the action (line 3: "A GREAT CATCH BY MACKENZIE"), and asserts MacKenzie's control over the result unequivocally (line 6: "Give MacKenzie all of the credit for that one"). Then, in interpreting the action, P_2 specifies the basis on which agency and control was awarded: the player's "<u>real real</u> concentration on the ball" (lines 8–9), a reference to both the <u>effort</u> and <u>intentions</u> of MacKenzie. The color broadcaster for Booth 2 (hereafter C_2), elaborates on other such evidence for positioning MacKenzie as accountable for what happened (in lines 13–19): The player "wanted" the ball, and "the only thing in the wor:ld that, mattered to Dwight MacKenzie was that <u>foot</u>ball no matter <u>who</u> was on." P_2 then continues giving MacKenzie credit on the basis of effort and intentions by stating that "MacKenzie just outfought 'im [the defender] for it" (lines 20–21).

Now consider the same play as it was called in Booth 1. Note that the partisan aspect is reversed: For the broadcasters in Booth 1 the play has a considerable negative outcome. The broadcasters deflect praise from, and blame, the agents involved in the action by calling attention to their physical attributes, much weaker grounds for ascribing creditable responsibility than effort and intentions.

(5) (Booth 1: home team = Broncos, other team = Vandals) [1:406–416]

```
 1   P₁:   ... =back to pass no:w is Hisa:w (0.7) and he's <firing
 2          long>,=the Broncos have a defender down there Jason
 3          Pay:ne=went! for the interception, didn't get it, Dwight
 4          MacKenzie comes down with the catch.
 5          (.)
 6   P₁:   Well a mis<u>take</u>! by Jason. Jason went for the interception
 7          (.) MacKenzie is taller than Payne just took the ball away
 8          from him, and the first big mistake of the afternoo:n.
 9   C₁:   We:ll >the thing of it< is, Paul you couldn't guard a guy
10          any better than <Jason Payne did> he just <u>didn't</u> execute
11          when the ball got there.
12          (.)
13   C₁:   He had 'im covered <perfectly, <u>just didn't get</u>> the ball
14          done.
15   P₁:   Well thrown ball by <u>Hisa</u>:w, first down at the:: Bronco
16          thirty four yard line.
```

Here P_1, in the real-time description (lines 1–4), identifies two players as agents in the action: the home team player, Payne, who "went! for the interception, didn't get it"; and MacKenzie, the receiver for the other team who "comes down with the catch." Note the consequence of this event for the partisan narrative: Because the play constitutes an exceptionally negative outcome for the home team, attributing agency means blaming the home team player, praising the other team player, or both—all of which undermine the broadcasters' partisan agenda. Accordingly, the partisan agenda is better served by suppressing the agency of the players. P_1 suppresses the agency of Payne, the home team player, by not detailing the maneuvers that led to Payne's failure to get the ball. Similarly, in stating that MacKenzie came down with the football, P_1 also avoids describing how MacKenzie accomplished the catch. Although P_1 awards agency to both players in the interpretive commentary (lines 6–9) (by attributing a mistake to Payne and stating that MacKenzie "just took the ball away from him") of interest is the way in which control of the action is accounted for. The action occurred, and both players are agents of it, only by virtue of a height difference: "MacKenzie is taller than Payne" (line 7). This serves to mitigate both blame and praise: Just as Payne has no control over his height disadvantage and cannot reasonably be blamed for it, MacKenzie's success is owing to a height advantage over which he has no control and for which he cannot be praised. The contribution by C_1 also serves the partisan agenda, as he praises the home team defender for guarding the other team receiver as well as possible (effort), stating that he simply didn't make the play once the ball arrived (lines 10–12, 14–15). Note that the agency of MacKenzie for making the catch is withheld in this comment by C_1, as well as in the next utterance in which he offers an upgraded attribution of Payne's skill ("had 'im covered <perfectly," in line 14).

In identifying agents of the action, establishing agency on the basis of effort and intentions may be equivocal. Even under the circumstances of this broadcast, in which there exists a motivation for and an expectation of partisanship, the broadcasters must support their attributions with evidence from the action they describe and interpret. Thus, in constructing a partisan narrative of the action, the broadcasters draw on the action itself to support their attributions to the effort and intentions of the players. Consider excerpt (6) following, from Booth 1. Here the home team quarterback for Booth 1, Hilde, is tackled by other team players after he makes a short gain.

(6) (Booth 1: home team = Broncos, other team = Vandals) [1:21–32]

```
 1  P₁:   First play of the ga:me, from scrimmage, it's an
 2         option,=Hilde keeps it he:'s across the thirty, backs
 3         his way to the thirty-two where he's hit <really
 4         ha:rd> (.) and goes down with a four yard gain, maybe
 5         a three yard gain.
 6         (1.2)
 7  C₁:   Jason O'Neil the defensive back came in=Tony (0.2) was
 8         kinda being drug down by somebody e:lse, >and O'Neil<
 9         came in there and really just rammed him <right in the
10         ba:ck>=  ⌜(>and en<)⌝
11  P₁:            ⌊    ye⌉ah one hold 'im ↑up, the other
12         one hit 'im.
13  C₁:   Yeah that's pretty much a <one two punch>.
14  P₁:   The: ol' <tag team wrest>ling move, right in the
15         kidneys.
```

In the real-time description, P_1 describes the home team quarterback (Hilde) as getting "hit <really ha:rd>" (lines 3–4) by an unnamed agent. In the interpretive commentary, C_1 identifies the agent of the action as O'Neil, a player for the other team. C_1 and then P_1 go on to provide evidence of O'Neil's effort and intention to hit hard. C_1 states that O'Neil "really just rammed him [Hilde] <right in the ba:ck>" while someone else was making the tackle (lines 8–10). P_1 then implies that the other team players made an effort to inflict violence on Hilde: He says that an opposing player held Hilde up so that O'Neil could hit him (lines 11–12). P_1 then compares this act to a "<tag-team wrest>ling move" (lines 14–15), alluding to a sport where violence is intentional and teammates collude unfairly to inflict extra harm on their opponents. With this allusion, P_1 implies that the players for the other team intentionally colluded to inflict harm.

In this section I have shown how the broadcasters construct a partisan narrative through account making: They assign agency or withhold it and cite evidence that magnifies or diminishes the players' responsibilities for the results of their actions on the field. In this way they are able to upgrade the praise of their home team players and mitigate blame, and conversely, mitigate praise of the opposing team and upgrade blame. In the following section I show ways in which the broadcasters in each of the broadcast booths coordinate and adhere to localized turn-taking conventions in order to coconstruct a partisan narrative. I then show how these coordination conventions—interaction constraints—are consequential to the partisan narrative.

COORDINATION BETWEEN THE BROADCASTERS

The broadcasters' first priority is to describe the action in real time. Other activities, such as interpreting the action just described, are contingent on whether there is action on the field, how soon action is to resume, and so forth. Thus, access to the floor is unequal between the broadcasters: The play-by-play broadcaster has primary access to the floor to describe the action in real time, and the color broadcaster has access to the floor only during the interval between plays. Contributions to the partisan narrative by the color broadcaster generally do not occur before the first turn relevance-place (TRP) after the play-by-play broadcaster describes the real-time action as having ended.

The play-by-play broadcaster's claim to the floor thus begins when he starts to describe the action on the field pursuant to the next play in the game and continues until after he describes that play as completed. However, even though the activity external to the sportscasters' booth—the action on the field of play independent of the talk—drives the description of the action in real time (see Kuiper, 1996), including its inception and completion, it does not fully control it. Of particular relevance here (even in [American] football which comprises a series of plays that start and stop) is that locating the "beginning" and "end" of action pursuant to a play is more complex than might at first be apparent. According to the rules of the game, a play begins when the offensive team puts the ball in play and ends when the referee blows the whistle to signal the end of the play. However, integral to real-time description in the broadcast data are descriptions of action before the offense puts the ball in play (substitutions, last-second line changes and player movement, etc.) as well as descriptions of action occurring after the referee's whistle (fights, injuries, penalties, etc.). Thus, for the analyst, the most appropriate definition of the "beginning" or "end" of action pursuant to a play is what the play-by-play broadcaster constructs it as being by what he (or she) begins talking about in resuming a description of action on the field after description of the prior play has ended and what he (or she) last describes after the next play has ended. As a result, the play-by-play broadcaster has some discretion about when the description of action on the field is resumed, because in doing so he (or she) reclaims sole access to the floor and ends color commentary.

Speaker change after action on the field has "ended" normally occurs by either self- or other-selection at TRPs in the talk. As in all turn-allocation systems in which there are multiple slots where a change in speakership could occur, the cooperation of the other, the color broadcaster, is needed. This cooperation does not appear to be worked out locally, but to utilize a standardized procedure, based on the institutional relationship between the play-by-play and color broadcasters.[3]

Although the real-time description is preallocated to the play-by-play broadcaster, coordination of turns at speaking between the two broadcasters in providing interpretive commentary is needed. Whereas the color broadcaster does not have access to the floor during real-time description and may contribute to the partisan narrative only in the interpretive commentary, the play-by-play broadcaster does have access to the floor during the color commentary between plays. During the interpretive commentary, the give-and-take between the broadcasters can resemble turn-taking in mundane conversation in which speaker change occurs at TRPs in the talk and in which either speaker may self-select to gain the floor (see Sacks, Schegloff, & Jefferson, 1974). Interpretive commentary ends when the play-by-play broadcaster reclaims the floor to describe the action in real time. In this manner, providing real-time description can be seen as a device by which the play-by-play broadcaster asserts his sole claim to the floor and maintains it across possible completion points in his description.

In the remainder of this section I compare conventions in the two booths for how the broadcasters coordinate to make the transition from real-time description to interpretive commentary and their allocation of turns at speaking (their division of labor) in providing the interpretive commentary itself. This is a precursor to the following section, in which I show how differences in the turn-taking procedure between the two broadcast booths are consequential for the coherence of the partisan narrative they respectively provide.

Transitions Between Real-Time Description and Interpretive Commentary

Because the color broadcaster has access to the floor only between plays, for the duration of the interpretive commentary, the first opportunity for a speaker change is at the transition from real-time description to interpretive commentary. The "shape" (see Pomerantz, 1987; see also Pomerantz, 1984) of the real-time description may play an important role in whether a speaker change occurs at this transition: Not only does this transition point constitute a recognizable end to the real-time narrative, but the end of the real-time description may be designed to select the color broadcaster as the next speaker. In this section I show how the broadcasters in each of the broadcast booths employed a similar convention—the "play–game summary"—to mark a transition point between the two activities of real-time description and interpretive commentary. I show how the convention had very different implications for how turns at speaking were allocated.

Summaries are frequently positioned at points of transition from real-time description to the interpretive commentary and back to real-time description. First, the "play summary" is a summary of the play just ended and a statement of its consequence to the game. This includes identifying the yard marker at which the play ended, stating how much yardage (toward reaching the goal line) was gained or lost in the play, reporting what "down" (first through fourth) the next play would be, the number of yards remaining to earn a new first down, and so forth. Second, the "game summary" consists of the current score, the time elapsed or remaining, and so forth. Two features of the play–game summary indicate that it is a powerful coordination device in the broadcast data considered here: First, although not always offered in a given play, it is invariably the play-by-play broadcaster who offers it; and second, it occurs at points in the broadcast talk where the color commentator's access to the floor starts or ends. Note in excerpt (7) following, P_1's control of the floor begins at line 5 with a play–game summary and is sustained during description of action on the field until the next play–game summary at lines 24–25, which is followed by a change in speakership.

(7) (Booth 1: home team = Boise State Broncos) [1:82–116]

1	C_1:		Well they're number one against the rush, they're only
2			allowing eight two yards rushing but Boise State feels
3			in order to be <u>success</u>ful (.) they have to establish
4			<some kind> of a rushing game.
5	P_1:	→	No sc↓ore twelve >and a half< minutes left to go first
6			quarter <u>no</u> gain on the >play it's< third down and
7			<u>two</u>:.
8			(1.7)

9	P_1:	Br<u>e</u>kke comes out of the lineup, the big freshman for
10		Boise State,=the Broncos will throw in an extra
11		receiver.
12		(0.7)
13	P_1:	Akebe and Richmond are balanced receivers,=see if
14		Idaho comes with their eight-man front,=they do not.
15		(2.0)
16	P_1:	↑ Well they're gettin clo:se.
17		(2.0)
18	P_1:	Hilde calling signals, (.) <u>very</u> n<u>oi</u>sy in here (0.7)
19		and the fans all received notices to make noise on
20		third do:wn.
21	P_1:	Screen pass (0.5) it's caught by R<u>ich</u>mond >breaks a
22		tackle he's to the fifty<, first down at the forty
23		five, bumped >out of bounds<, at the Vandal forty one
24	→	yard line, and the Broncos keep the opening <drive
25		ali::ve> on the Vandal forty one.
26		(0.2)
27	C_1:	What a great first move by uh (.) Richmond after he
28		caught the ball, >but the big thing< that made that
29		play work, (.) Idaho came, and (.) gambled on defense,
30		brought the blitz, Boise State had the middle screen-
31		actually the- ah: a kind of a flanker screen goin
32		there, and (.) n<u>i</u>ce move by Richmond.

As illustrated in this insert, the play–game summary is a coordinating device that marks the transition from real-time description to interpretive commentary and from interpretive commentary back to real-time description. The first play–game summary (lines 5–7) marks the beginning of the real-time description, in which P_1 has sole access to the floor even across notable pauses in the talk (lines 8, 12, 15, and 17). Similarly, the play–game summary marks the end of the real-time description (lines 24–25), at which point C_1 takes the floor to provide interpretive commentary (in lines 27–32).

The play–game summary is utilized similarly in Booth 2: It is invariably offered by the play-by-play broadcaster and occurs at transition points between real-time description and color commentary. This is illustrated in excerpt (8).

(8) (Booth 2: home team = Vandals; other team = Broncos) [2:310–337]

```
 1   P₂:        A:nd the Broncos keep it, they come up (1.5) both uh
 2              tight ends line up <to the left> (0.5) and to the
 3              short side of the field, single running back is Aid-
 4              Adams.
 5              (.)
 6   P₂:        Now Aikebe's in motion to the right, (.) as Hilde on
 7              the quarterback draw right >up the< middle across
 8   →         the midfield stripe (0.2) may have got enough to=uh:
 9              for the first down (0.2) as he di:ves forward to the
10              Vandal forty seven.
11              (.)
12   P₂:        Hilde is, a:ll of the offense for <Boise State> (.)
13              and the Vandals are grabbin' at 'im they- but they
14              can't get anything but ai:r.
15   C₂:        I think they:, they knew he could run it, but you
16              know (0.2) ↑playin em is a different thing.=He is
17              very very quick,=good athle:te, (0.5) the offensive
18              line all five starters come back from last year's,
19              uh: runner up team 'n' (.) they're doin' a pretty
20              good job up there spreadin out Idaho's defense as
21              well as (m)akin' the power play >straight up the
22              ↑middle<.
23   P₂:   →   First down and ten to go:, Merlin Carey comes in as
24              another running back, let's put im down 'ere
25              somewhere, as a slot formation (.) as Hilde keeps it
26              ((description of action on the field continues))
```

Similarly to Booth 1, the play–game summaries occur at transition points in the talk. The first arrow, line 8 in excerpt (8), marks the use of a summary at the transition from real-time description to interpretive commentary: "may have got enough to=uh: for the first down (0.2) as he di:ves forward to the Vandal forty seven" (lines 8–10). The second arrow (line 23) marks the play–game summary at the transition point from interpretive commentary back to real-time description.

Because it is invariably positioned at transition points between types of talk (description versus commentary), the play–game summary is recognizable as constituting the end of one type and the beginning of the other. The play–game summary worked similarly in both broadcast booths to mark the end of interpretive commentary, in which both broadcasters have access to the floor, and the beginning of play-by-play description, in which P has sole access to the floor to describe action on the field. Similarly, the play–game summary marked the transition from real-time description to interpretive commentary in both broadcast booths. Despite the uniform positioning of the play–game summary, this convention had very different implications for speaker change, at the transition from real-time description to interpretive commentary, in the broadcast booths. While C_1 took the floor following 16 of 21 real-time descriptions that ended with a play–game summary, C_2 took the floor following only 6 of 19 real-time descriptions that ended with a play–game summary.

The considerable difference between the two booths in managing changes in speakership at the transition from real-time description to interpretive commentary is also evident in instances where a play–game summary is not given at the end of the real-time description. Consider excerpts (9) and (10) following, which feature comparable real-time descriptions. In excerpt (9), from Booth 2, the broadcasters' home team is on defense; Adams plays for the other team, and Ryan Phillips plays for the home team. The end of the real-time description is marked with an arrow in the transcript.

(9) (Booth 2: home team = Vandals, other team = Broncos) [2:69–83]

1	P₂:	Broncos break out (.) still: uh (2.0) Aikebe goes wide
2		>to the left, wide to the right< is: uh: (0.2)
3		Richmond.
4		(1.2)
5	P₂:	A <u>pro</u> set now, split running backs <Adams and Craven>.
6		(1.2)
7	P₂:	An:d the handoff goes to Adams, Adams hits the right
8	→	side and he:: (0.2) hits Ryan Phillips.
9		(0.2)
10	P₂:	<When you hit> Ryan Phillips you're not gonna go
11		<u>any</u>where.
12		(0.2)
13	P₂:	And Phillips just bounced im back=had some help, from
14		<u>M</u>itchell and Wilson,=they were all the:re.
15		(0.2)
16	P₂: →	So no:w, it's third down 'n ↑eight (.) and it's gonna
17		be a definite passing situation (.) for the: uh-

18   Bronco:s, and Mike Richmond comes in . . . ((*continues*
19   *real-time description*))

In the preceding excerpt, P_2, in describing the unfolding action and the end
of the play, states simply that the player for the other team "hits Ryan
Phillips," the home team player (line 8). P_2 implies that the play ended (by
not continuing with the narrative), but is not explicit in describing the end
of the play and does not offer a play summary. Instead, he promptly begins
a commentary (lines 10–15) that concludes, with a play–game summary
(line 16), all without the participation of the color broadcaster.

Conversely, the broadcasters in Booth 1, excerpt (10) following,
manage a speaker change at the end of the description of action on the
field despite the lack of a play–game summary or other component to
mark the completion of real-time description (except perhaps the gap at
line 7). In this excerpt the home team for the broadcasters is on offense.
Karlin Adams is the home team player who carries the ball.

(10) (Booth 1: home team = Boise State; other team = Vandals) [1:77–88]

1   P_1:   Gain of two: second down and eight yards to go for
2   Boise State split running backs (0.7) Karlin Adams and
3   Graven Brekke, the tight end in motion.
4   (1.0)
5   P_1:   Vandals in a zone >defense hand< off to Karlin Adams,
6   there is no hole.
7   (2.7)
8   C_1:   Well they're number one against the rush, they're only
9   allowing eighty two yards rushing but Boise State
10   feels in order to be successful (.) they have to
11   establish <some kind> of a rushing game.
12 P_1:   No sc↓ore twelve >and a half< minutes left to go first
13   quarter no gain on the >play it's< third down and
14   two:.

In describing the unfolding action and the end of the play, P_1 states simply
that "there is no hole" (line 6), meaning that the home team player Adams
had no place to run with the ball. Similarly to excerpt (9), neither an explicit
reference to the end of the play nor a play summary is provided. However,
contrary to Booth 2, C_1 self-selects to provide interpretive commentary.
Although pause length was not found to be a pervasive feature of coordi-

nation at transition points in the talk, the considerable gap at line 7 shows how P_1 may cooperate in effecting a speaker change at the transition point, by withholding commentary until C_1 takes the floor.

While C_1 took the floor at the first TRP following the real-time description in 24 of 39 plays in the corpus, C_2 took the floor at the first TRP following real-time description in only 9 of 39 plays. This tendency in Booth 1 for C_1 to take the floor at the first TRP following real-time description, whether the end of that description is marked with a play–game summary or not, indicates the significant role of the observable action on the field in the coordination between the broadcasters. Unlike previous analyses of turn taking in institutional realms—such as news interviews (Greatbatch, 1988; Heritage & Roth, 1995), court proceedings (Atkinson, 1992; Drew, 1992; Philips, 1992), job interviews (Button, 1992) and radio talk shows (Gaik, 1992; Hutchby, 1996)—sports broadcasters orient to an external event in addition to the talk (Kuiper, 1996), and this has a material effect on access to the floor and changes in speakership.

As noted earlier, a speaker change at the transition from real-time description to interpretive commentary was characteristic of Booth 1, regardless of the shape of the real-time description. In Booth 2, a speaker change at that juncture was uncharacteristic, despite turn shapes that marked a transition from real-time description to interpretive commentary similarly to those in Booth 1. The pervasive differences between the booths in this regard has consequences for the coherence of the partisan narrative that each booth produces, and the coordination of the sportscasters in producing that narrative.

Coordination in Providing Interpretive Commentary

In excerpt (9) above, C_2 does not contribute to the narrative in the interval between episodes of action described in real time. This was not irregular in Booth 2: Whereas C_1 provided commentary at some point in the interval between all 39 plays in the corpus, C_2 only provided commentary at some point in the interval between only 25 of those 39 plays. Correspondingly, P_1 produced about 66% of the total broadcast talk in Booth 1, and P_2 provided about 82% of the broadcast talk in Booth 2.[4]

As noted previously, whether a speaker change occurs at the transition from real-time description to interpretive commentary was often, but not always, related to the shape of the real-time description. Conversely, when speaker change did not occur at this transition, the shape of the interpretive commentary that the play-by-play broadcaster went on to produce did influence whether the color commentator also took a turn at speaking before the next episode of action in real time began. Consider excerpt (11) following, from Booth 1. Here the broadcasters' home team has the ball, and the quarterback Tony Hilde attempts a forward pass to the home team receiver Richmond.

(11) (Booth 1: home team = Broncos; other team = Vandals) [1:410–425]

```
 1   P₁:   Zimmerman resets, right to left, Broncos driving,
 2         first do:wn, at the, forty four in Vandal territory,
 3         no score, four twenty left to go, first half=Hilde,
 4         conventional drop, he's hit, breaks a↑wa:y: (.) a::nd
 5         now >fires downfield,=got! a man out there< Richmond
 6         he came back in bounds he was an ineligible receiver
 7         anyway (0.2) and a penalty flag is down,=Hilde <got
 8         cre::amed>
 9         (1.0)
10   P₁:   He rea:!lly got hit hard.
11         (1.5)
12   P₁:   And the Vandal fans are cheering.
13         (0.2)
14   P₁:   Boy these guys are dogs=
15   C₁:   =Well <Dave Longoria> is the guy that hit 'im after he
16         threw the ball and ⌈had to p⌉ull awa:y
17   P₁:                      ⌊No fla:gs!⌋
18         (0.5)
19   P₁:   Got 'im in the hea:d
20         (1.7)
21   P₁:   with uh one of these=u:h (0.2) forearm shivers.
```

In the preceding excerpt, P₁ describes the unfolding action as well as the end of the play: Hilde "fires downfield" to Richmond (line 5), who by virtue of having left the field of play (having gone out of bounds) was an ineligible receiver, even if he had caught the ball. (That he didn't catch the ball is implied by "anyway" in line 7: "He was an ineligible receiver anyway.") P₁ then adds that the referees had thrown a penalty marker onto the field, and in a latched statement offers an interpretation of the action: "Hilde <got cre::amed>" (lines 7–8).

Because it is the first TRP following the description of action in real-time, the TRP at "cre::amed" (line 8) marks the transition from real-time description to interpretive commentary in which a speaker change could occur. However, C_1 does not take the floor. Here P_1 adds a series of three assessments, each followed by a slot in which a speaker change could occur. Latched to the third assessment ("Boy these guys are dogs" in line 14), C_1 then does take a turn and contributes to the interpretive commentary. As noted previously, this delay in change of speakership after the end of real-time description was unusual in Booth 1: C_1 took the floor at the first TRP following real-time description in 27 of 39 plays. Excerpt (11) preceding is typical of the other 12 plays in that even when he delayed doing so, there was ample opportunity for C_1 to take the floor at some point in the interpretive commentary (which he did in all 39 plays).

However, the organization of the talk in the interpretive commentary was very different in Booth 2. C_2 took the floor at the transition from real-time description to interpretive commentary in only 10 of the 39 plays. Furthermore, of the remaining 29 plays, C_2 took the floor at some point in the interpretive commentary in only 15. Consider excerpt (12) following, from Booth 2. Here the broadcasters' home team for Booth 2 is on defense. The other team attempts a forward pass, but O'Neil, a player for the home team, knocks the ball away from the opposition.

(12) (Booth 2: home team = Vandals; other team = Broncos) [2:135–154]

```
 1   P₂:   Now it's third down and about ↑ooh: eighteen nineteen
 2         to go:.
 3         (.)
 4   P₂:   Two wide receivers right, >one to the left<.
 5         (.)
 6   P₂:   The tight e:nd flip flops goes from left to right,=
 7         =single running back is Adams.
 8         (.)
 9   P₂:   Hilde back to pass. Hilde rolls to the right. Hilde
10         steps up (roils) to the left, now he (sets) throws
11         long, MAN DOWN THE::RE (0.2) it i::s knocked down at
12         the last moment at the five yard line (.) by Jason
13         O'Nei:l.
14         (0.2)
15   P₂:   Great great protection by O'Neil, who was back there
```

16   alo:ng (.) with the free safety (being) Travis Coffey,
17   (.) they're playing a zo:ne with a cover three defense
18   (.) and it paid off that time (.) as the receiver Ryan
19   Akebe was alone there for a moment but he had to wait
20   for the ball (.) enabling O'Neil to come over and
21   knock it away:, incomplete, it'll be fourth down and
22   nineteen to go, a kicking situation for the first time
23   (.) for Jeff Davis.=Single safety is Ted Seve:re (.)
24   standing on his own ten for the Vandals.=So the Vandal
25   defense stops the Bronco:s (.) and they're gonna have
26   to kick.

In this excerpt, P_2 describes the play as ending: The pass "i::s knocked down at the last moment at the five yard line (.) by Jason O'Nei:l.," a player for the home team (lines 11–13). At this TRP there is a transition to interpretive commentary, in which speaker change also could occur (and commonly does occur in Booth 1). Here speaker change does not occur. In contrast to excerpt (11)—in which P_1 offers three short assessments, each marked (by a sizable gap) for C_1 to contribute to the commentary—here no slot, and no gap, is made available for a speaker change. (The gap at line 27 occurs after a play–game summary has been given, twice, in lines 21–22 and 24–26, marking the resumption of real-time description.) Rather, P_2 provides the interpretive commentary (lines 15–21) in a single extended turn construction unit (Heritage & Roth, 1995; see also Sacks, Schegloff, & Jefferson, 1974).[5]

In this section I have compared the two booths in how the play-by-play broadcaster managed the transition from real-time description to interpretive commentary and shown how they differed in the allocation of speaking turns during the interpretive commentary itself. These differences suggest that the participation of C_1 was expected and integral to the creation of a partisan narrative, whereas the participation of C_2 was peripheral to the development of a partisan narrative. In particular, the narrative account of the action by the broadcasters in Booth 1 was interactively coconstructed by the two broadcasters to a greater extent than was the narrative account in Booth 2. The ongoing narrative in Booth 2 was, for the most part, constructed by the play-by-play broadcaster and merely decorated—or "colored"—by the color broadcaster.

Because C_1 had a more central role in the construction of the narrative account of the action than the color broadcaster in Booth 2, there existed in Booth 1 a greater risk of coordination trouble in providing a coherent, unified, partisan narrative. In the section that follows I show how inconsistencies in the partisan narrative sometimes arose between the two broadcasters, as well as how the broadcasters repaired them.

DISCREPANCIES IN A COCONSTRUCTED PARTISAN NARRATIVE

When the game is narrated by more than one broadcaster, discrepant versions of the narrative may emerge as the broadcasters coordinate to describe the action in real time and provide interpretive commentary of the action just concluded. These discrepancies may involve who is identified as the agent of the action, or the evidence adduced to show the degree of an agent's responsibility for the results of his action. In this section I show how discrepancies in the partisan narrative emerge and explicate how the broadcasters change, mitigate, and modify accounts in order to produce a unified, coherent, partisan narrative.

Discrepancies in Naming the Agent

Because any accountable action—praiseworthy or blameworthy—requires identification of the agent of the action, naming the agent is integral to the partisan narrative and a site of potential discrepancy. Consider excerpt (13) following, in which the home team quarterback runs for a first down. For the broadcasters in Booth 1, the play has a positive outcome. A discrepancy emerges as to whom the agent responsible for the action is, which surfaces in the form of a short-lived dispute.

(13) (Booth 1: home team = Broncos, other team = Idaho Vandals) [1:50–64]

```
1   P₁:   Hilde rolling out, option play keeps it, has the first
2         down, breaks a tackle across the forty to the forty
3         four yard line.
4         (1.2)
5   C₁:   Broncos ran to the weak si:de.
6         (.)
7   C₁:   You know I tell you what:, uh (.) Idaho (.) they- I
```

8   guess Northern Iowa, the coaching staff saw a lo:tta
9   different things about (.) when they overload on one
10   side de<u>fen</u>sively and Boise State <u>ran</u> da (.) the
11   Vandals weak side 'n'=
12   P_1:   =Did you see the <u>hand</u> signal by Hilde? behind his <u>back</u>
13   ┌(.) sayin which way┐ he was gonna go.
14   C_1:   └Exactly (0.2) yeah┘
15   C_1:   He was <u>showin</u> 'em that he <u>read</u> that he picked it up
16   that's >some of the< stuff they talked at back at the
17   hot<u>el</u>.

In describing the action, P_1 identifies the home team quarterback, Hilde, as
the agent of the favorable outcome (lines 1–3). However, in the interpretive
commentary, C_1 identifies the home team coaching staff as responsible for
the positive outcome by explaining (in lines 7–11) that the weakness in the
opposing team that Hilde exploited had been identified by the coaching staff
through analysis of the opposing team's previous game against Northern
Iowa. P_1 responds by reasserting Hilde as the agent of the action. He does
this by calling attention to Hilde's hand signal prior to the play that indicated
which way he would run (lines 12–13). C_1 displays unequivocal agreement
with the observation made by P_1, then brings the two (up to this point)
discordant observations to accord by characterizing Hilde as the "conduit"
through which the coaching staff's finding was incorporated in the team's
play, stating that Hilde's signal was the result of something he learned
earlier from his coaches (lines 15–17).

Here the discord between the broadcasters in naming the agent (Hilde
versus the home team coaching staff) produces not only a discrepancy
in the narrative of the action but one with consequences for where Hilde
could be positioned in the developing partisan narrative of the game. The
discrepancy emerges owing to the coequal participation of the broadcasters in identifying the agent of the action. On the other hand, when naming
the agent is not in question, a discrepancy is less likely to emerge. Consider
excerpt (14) following, from Booth 2. Here the opposing team is on
offense, and the opposing quarterback (Hilde) is tackled by Sheltz, a
home team player.

(14) (Booth 2: home team = Vandals, other team = Broncos) [2:13–23]

1   P_2:   It's a slot eye formation, double tight ends four man
2   front Hilde rolls out cuts it back and=he's hit by

3   Sheltz and knocked down after he picks up maybe a
4   coupler three yards.
5   (2.0)
6 P₂: They like tuh do that a lot Tom,=Tony Hilde will keep
7   it on an option, he just took it out under center,
8   rolled to his right tried to pick up a little bit,
9   picked >up a cuppla< yards (.) but Jason Sheltz was
10   waitin' for him.=
11 C₂: =He was there to close the door, Sheltz put out his
12   right arm and wrapped him up there then brought him
13   down >with the help< of the interior defense, but not
14   much gain.

In describing the play, two agents are offered by P₂ (lines 1–4): the opposing quarterback (Hilde), and the home team player (Sheltz). Because speaker change did not occur at the transition from real-time description (ending in line 4) to interpretive commentary (beginning in line 6), P₂ offers the initial interpretation of the action. In the interpretive commentary, P₂ establishes a weak basis for Hilde's agency, characterizing the action as mere tendency or habit of the team ("They like tuh do that a lot" in line 6). P₂ establishes the agency of Sheltz, the home team player, on a much stronger basis—intention—by describing Sheltz as "waitin' for him" (Hilde; lines 9–10). Having been cued to take a turn at speaking (in line 6 in which P₂ names C₂ as recipient of his current turn), with the agent of the action already named for him, C₂ elaborates the narrative as it had been started, focusing on Sheltz's role in producing the outcome (lines 11–14).

Note that factors other than turn taking, such as the willingness of C₂ to "go along" with the partisan narrative as it is constructed by P₂, might also make a difference in whether a discrepancy occurs. The argument here is not that C₂ was precluded from calling into question the identification of the agent or the basis for agency. Instead, it is that the turn-taking convention in Booth 2—in which a speaker change did not generally occur at the transition from real-time description to interpretive commentary—gives the play-by-play broadcaster the opportunity to shape the partisan narrative to constrain the color broadcaster. This reduces the likelihood that discrepant versions will emerge in identifying the agent as the broadcasters interpret the action just concluded.

Discrepancies in the Magnitude of Attributed Responsibility

The expression of partisanship not only depends on awarding or denying agency, but as discussed earlier, it also depends on how much the agent is held responsible for the result of his actions, based on whether the agent's responsibility for the results of his actions is attributed to his resources and experience or his effort and intentions. Accordingly, the evidence of accountability is also a site of potential discrepancy in the partisan narrative, as illustrated by excerpt (15) following, from Booth 1. The home team, Broncos, fail to complete a pass amid expectations for success created in the description of the action. The partisan broadcasters mitigate the blame of home team players.

(15) (Booth 1: home team = Broncos, other team = Vandals) [1:146–162]

```
 1   P₁:   So the Broncos with not much ti:me here on
 2         offense=here comes the spread offense again.
 3         (2.5)
 4   P₁:   The crowd tryin >to get< into it, Zimmerman resets (.)
 5         on the near si:de.
 6         (1.2)
 7   P₁:   Hilde ro:lling out (0.2) here comes the ru:sh, steps
 8         >up in the< pocket, now has all day=has ti:me ↑firi:ng
 9         HE'S GOT A MAN WIDE OPEN AKEB:E! (0.2) HE dropped the
10         ba:ll=it >might have been< knocked away at the last
11         minute by the Vandal defender.
12         (.)
13   C₁:   Yeah, it was knocked away,=it never got to Ryan.
14         (.)
15   C₁:   ┌But Ake-┐
16   P₁:   └  Bo:y  ┘ was  he wide open.
17   C₁:   Yeah a good job by ah (0.2) Tony: and really I- I'm
18         surpri:sed Tony underthrew it,=I mean, (.) Tony I've
19         seen him throw sixty ya:rds, and that time he only
20         threw it about fifty, and (0.2) he just under threw
21         it.
22         (0.5)
23   P₁:   Well, the Broncos had a shot, really the ti:ming <was
24         all> screwed up (0.2) and ah: you know threw it late
```

25   and the Vandals had time to recover, but ↑boy Akebe
26   was <<u>wi</u>:de <u>open</u>>.

In describing the action in real time, P_1 creates formidable expectations for
success by the home team, by stating that Hilde is not being threatened by
defensive players and has plenty of time ("now has all day=has ti:me" in
line 8), and that Akebe, the home team receiver, is in a position to receive
the pass because no defenders are near him ("HE'S GOT A MAN WIDE
OPEN" in line 9). As the action unfolds and the play fails (by virtue of the
pass going uncaught), P_1 identifies Akebe as the agent of the blameworthy
act of dropping the ball (lines 9–10: "HE dropped the ba:ll"), then quickly
reverses field and tentatively assigns agency to a player for the other team
(lines 10–11: "it might have been knocked away"). C_1 affirms the second
attribution (line 13: "Yeah, it was knocked away"), joining in deflecting
blame away from Akebe. However, P_1 then implicates Hilde, the home team
quarterback, as blameworthy by reiterating (line 16) that Akebe was wide
open: By reiterating this, P_1 makes it puzzling how the ball could have been
knocked away if no defenders were around, unless the ball had not been
thrown as directly to Akebe by Hilde as it should have been. Shifting the
blame toward Hilde in that way is at odds with the partisan agenda of
accounting for the failed play—which had been characterized in the
real-time description as potentially a great success—while portraying the
home team and its players in the most favorable light possible.

C_1 attempts to mitigate the blame that P_1 tacitly shifted to Hilde by
stating that Hilde's performance in this instance was an anomaly—it was
incongruous with his overall physical ability (lines 18–20: "I've seen him
throw sixty ya:rds, and that time he only threw it about <u>fifty</u> (0.2) and
he just under th<u>rew</u> it"). This is prefaced with considerable work to
mitigate blame: praising Hilde outright ("a good job," line 17), and
expressing surprise that the ball was underthrown (lines 17–18). Yet P_1
in response undermines this and amplifies his criticism of Hilde: "Really
the <u>ti</u>:ming <was all> screwed up (0.2) and ah: you know th<u>rew</u> it late"
(lines 23–24), attributing agency to Hilde for the failed play ("you know
th<u>rew</u> it late," line 24), and ascribing the failure not to ability but effort,
enhancing Hilde's blameworthiness. At the same time, P_1 mitigates this
renewed blame by using the passive voice ("timing was all screwed up")
thereby avoiding direct mention of any one agent of the failed play. Even
shifting to an active construction, P_1 continues to avoid a direct reference
to Hilde as the agent of the failed play by simply leaving the agent slot
blank in this odd active construction: "you know th<u>rew</u> it late."

In this excerpt, a discrepancy emerges as the broadcasters construct a partisan narrative to mitigate Hilde's agency. Although both broadcasters identify Hilde as the agent of the action, they differ on the way in which blameworthiness is deflected away from Hilde or reduced: C_1 characterized Hilde's displayed lack of physical skill as an anomaly, whereas P_1, though blaming the failure on insufficient effort by Hilde, avoided direct reference to Hilde as the agent.

Excerpts (13) and (15) in this section illustrate that discrepancies in the partisan narrative may occur as the broadcasters identify the agent of the action and indicate what degree of responsibility he has for the result of his actions. Excerpt (14) illustrates that a discrepancy in the partisan narrative is less likely to occur if it is mainly one person, in this case the play-by-play broadcaster, who both identifies the agent and evidence of the agent's degree of accountability prior to the color broadcaster's turn at speaking. This is not a claim about the broadcasters themselves, but a claim about the turn-taking conventions utilized by a pair of broadcasters. When the turn-taking convention gives both broadcasters equal access to the floor in the interval between plays, as in Booth 1, the chances are greater that differing ways of constructing the partisan narrative will arise. In the ensuing effort to assert one version over the other, or to reconcile them, a different partisan narrative may result than had there been a single, dominant version in the first place.

DISCUSSION

This is not the first study that has recognized that sports broadcasts are biased. However, this study has dealt with specific ways in which bias is expressed, introducing the way accounts are formulated as a previously unexamined means of allocating praise and blame. In addition, this study brings to the surface a dimension that previous studies of broadcasting have overlooked: that, when two or more broadcasters are involved, producing an internally consistent game narrative in real time is a coordinated achievement by the broadcasters.

This study has considered partisanship as it is expressed through the broadcasters' attributions of agency to players for accountable actions—either praiseworthy or blameworthy—and the kind of evidence they cite for holding an agent accountable. However, there are numerous other ways of expressing partisanship in sports broadcasts. Unlike the focus here on radio, most previous work has focused on the expression of partisanship on television through devices such as on-screen graphics, camera angles, and other methods such as video editing in providing recaps of events and creating "character portraits" (Messner, Duncan, & Jensen, 1993), pre- and post-game interviews with athletes (Daddario, 1994; Emmison, 1987, 1988), and "compensatory rhetoric" (Daddario, 1994). Much research about bias in sportscasting has been produced because of a specific concern with gender bias. This research has explored the expression of such bias through linguistic devices such as: *asymmetrical naming,* specifically using different naming conventions for men versus women (Halbert & Latimer, 1994; Messner et al., 1993; Weidman, 1997); using *"marked forms"* to refer to women's sports and women athletes (Messner et al., 1993; Weidman, 1997); *differing ratios of praise to criticism* allocated to men and women in a mixed gender event (Halbert & Latimer, 1994); and referring to women, but not men, with *"infantilizing" descriptors* (Halbert & Latimer, 1994; Weidman, 1997).

However, as noted previously, this work has overlooked the broadcasters' problem of achieving a coherent, partisan narrative in real time. This may be due to the general tendency in these studies to rely on coding and content analysis, and to not examine the sequential and localized nature of broadcast talk. Deconstructing the naturalistic data themselves, and considering partisanship as expressed through account making, allow not only an appreciation of the intricacies with which agency is selected and attributed, but an understanding of the coordination between the broadcasters to achieve a coherent partisan narrative. The conversation analytic perspective, which focuses on the sequential organization of partisan narratives in sports broadcasts, allows this coordination problem to enter into the analysis. Considering sports broadcasts as giving accounts to construct a narrative of the action, and attending to the sequential organization of the broadcast data themselves, may enhance the findings of future analyses of this nature.

The preceding considerations leave the question of whether the sports broadcast structure of real-time description and interpretive commentary of the action just concluded (Ferguson, 1983; Kuiper, 1995) generalizes to sports other than American football. The game of football, which occurs in spurts of action followed by periods of lag time during which the teams reset for the next action episode, lends itself well to the broadcast structure of real-time description of the action followed by interpretive commentary of the action just concluded. Ferguson (1983) contended only that sports broadcasting consists of these two "phases of discourse"—with "interesting boundary phenomena" (p. 156) between them—which are characterized by different linguistic properties. Kuiper (1995), drawing on Ferguson and others to explicate the real-time description of a horse race, stated that this sports broadcast structure exists in the broadcast narratives of "ice hockey, basketball, cricket, football, and no doubt many other sports" (p. 10).

However, whether broadcast narratives of other sports follow the same structure is an open question. It is probable that narratives of games in team sports such as ice hockey, basketball, and soccer, in which the action is both fast and constant, are structured differently than football narratives. Narratives of "slow sports" such as cricket and baseball are likely to be structured differently as well. Considering that previous research has analyzed partisanship in basketball (Weidman, 1997), tennis (Halbert & Latimer, 1994), and various Olympic sports (Daddario, 1994), closer attention to how games are narrated across sports may be helpful in explicating how partisanship is achieved in sports broadcast talk.

In addition to the question of generalizing the sports broadcast structure to other sports, the structure considered in this study itself is worth continued scrutiny. In this study I have considered as different activities the real-time description of the action and the interpretation of the action in the interval between plays. Although not considered here, the question of how real-time descriptions constrain interpretations, and whether or not there is a description that is not also interpretive, is worth pursuing. For the purposes of this study I have left the relation largely unspecified, stating the narrative is developed and sustained primarily in the interpretive commentary, sometimes based on characterizations provided in the description of the unfolding action. Further inquiry into the organization of sports broadcasts, whether there is one broadcaster who performs both the play-by-play and the color commentary, or the tasks are divided, may attempt to specify the import of the real-time description on the narrative account.

NOTES

1   Because "even the simplest, most basic description . . . involves classifying it . . . with other things" (Trew, 1979, p. 96), Ferguson's (1983) discussion of play-by-play description and color commentary as separate activities may beg the question of

whether there exists a description that is not also interpretive. It is a question worth pursuing, which I discuss later, whether the descriptions provided by the play-by-play broadcasters are also interpretive and contribute to the emerging narrative of the game. However, the concerns of this study can best be pursued by upholding Ferguson's (1983) distinction, because considering description and interpretation as separate activities allows for a clearer discussion of the turn taking between the respective pairs of broadcasters.

2 In American football each team is allowed four "downs" or "plays" in which they must either achieve progress of at least 10 yards toward the goal line or turn over possession of the ball to the opposing team (shift from offense to defense). When 10 or more yards are earned, the team is awarded with a new first down, that is, four new opportunities to progress another 10 or more yards toward the goal line.

3 Although the sportscasters in this game utilized a regular turn-allocation system, the data are not strong enough to claim that there is a turn-taking system specific to sportscasting, akin to the system Greatbatch (1988) and others (see Clayman & Whalen, 1988/89; and Heritage & Roth, 1995) have identified for news interviews. Such a claim would require evidence of massive regularity and repair of departures from the system, which the data so far do not provide. Although they discussed regularities in sports broadcasting, neither Kuiper (1996) nor Ferguson (1983) made any claims regarding a turn-taking system. It may become more apparent in future research whether there is a turn-taking system in sports broadcasting.

4 The amount of broadcast talk provided by the broadcasters was measured by counting the total transcript lines (excluding talk occurring under the talk of the other) in each broadcast and calculating the proportion of those total lines produced by the play-by-play broadcaster in each booth. A t test reveals a significant difference (at $p < .001$) between the proportion of talk produced by the respective play-by-play broadcasters.

5 Although this is common in Booth 2 and typical of the Booth 2 broadcasters' coordination of turns at speaking, P_2 offering the interpretive commentary in a single turn construction unit was not the only turn shape that occurred in which C_2 did not contribute to the commentary. For instance, in excerpt (10), there are gaps of $\frac{2}{10}$ of a sec after two of P_2's assessments, at lines 12 and 15, in which speaker change could occur, but does not. The external activity—in this case the imminence of action to be described in real time, as perceived by both broadcasters—may play a role in whether C_2 contributes to the interpretive commentary.

REFERENCES

Atkinson, J. M. (1992). Displaying neutrality: Formal aspects of informal court proceedings. In P. Drew & J. Heritage (Eds.), *Talk at work: Interaction in institutional settings* (pp. 199–211). New York: Cambridge University Press.

Buttny, R. (1993). *Social accountability in communication.* Newbury Park, CA: Sage.

Button, G. (1992). Answers as interactional products: Two sequential practices used in job interviews. In P. Drew & J. Heritage (Eds.), *Talk at work: Interaction in institutional settings* (pp. 212–232). New York: Cambridge University Press.

Clayman, S. E., & Whalen, J. (1988/89). When the medium becomes the message: The case of the Rather–Bush encounter. *Research on Language and Social Interaction, 22,* 241–272.

Daddario, G. (1994). Chilly scenes from the 1992 Winter Games: The mass media and marginalization of female athletes. *Sociology of Sport Journal, 11,* 275–288.

Drew, P. (1992). Contested evidence in courtroom cross-examination: The case of a trial for rape. In P. Drew and J. Heritage (Eds.), *Talk at work: Interaction in institutional settings* (pp. 470–520). New York: Cambridge University Press.

Emmison, M. (1987). Victors and vanquished: The social organization of ceremonial congratulations and commiserations. *Language & Communication, 7,* 93–110.

Emmison, M. (1988). On the interactional management of defeat. *Sociology, 22,* 233–251.

Ferguson, C. A. (1983). Sports announcer talk: Syntactic aspects of register variation. *Language in Society, 12,* 153–172.

Gaik, F. (1992). Radio talk-show therapy and the pragmatics of possible worlds. In A. Duranti & C. Goodwin (Eds.), *Rethinking context: Language as an interactive phenomenon* (pp. 272–289). New York: Cambridge University Press.

Greatbatch, D. (1988). A turn-taking system for British news interviews. *Language and Society, 17,* 401–430.

Halbert, C., & Latimer, M. (1994). 'Battling' gendered language: An analysis of the language used by sports commentators in a televised coed tennis competition. *Sociology of Sport Journal, 11,* 298–308.

Heritage, J. C., & Roth, A. L. (1995). Grammar and institution: Questions and questioning in the broadcast news interview. *Research on Language and Social Interaction, 28,* 1–60.

Hutchby, I. (1996). *Confrontation talk: Arguments, asymmetries, and power on talk radio.* Mahwah, NJ: Lawrence Erlbaum Associates, Inc.

Kuiper, K. (1995). *Smooth talkers: The linguistic performance of auctioneers and sportscasters.* Mahwah, NJ: Lawrence Erlbaum Associates, Inc.

Messner, M. A., Duncan, M. C., & Jensen, K. (1993). Separating the men from the girls: The gendered language of televised sports. *Gender and Society, 7,* 121–137.

Philips, S. U. (1992). The routinization of repair in courtroom discourse. In A. Duranti & C. Goodwin (Eds.), *Rethinking context: Language as an interactive phenomenon* (pp. 312–322). New York: Cambridge University Press.

Pomerantz, A. (1984). Agreeing and disagreeing with assessments: Some features of preferred/dispreferred turn shapes. In J. M. Atkinson & J. Heritage (Eds.), *Structures of social action* (pp. 152–163). New York: Cambridge University Press.

Pomerantz, A. (1987). Descriptions in legal settings. In G. Button & J. R. E. Lee (Eds.), *Talk and social organisation* (pp. 226–243). Clevedon, England: Multilingual Matters.

Sacks, H., Schegloff, E. A., & Jefferson, G. (1974). A simplest systematics for the organization of turn-taking for conversation. *Language, 50,* 697–735.

Trew, T. (1979). Theory and ideology at work. In R. Fowler, B. Hodge, G. Kress, & T. Trew (Eds.), *Language and control* (pp. 94–116). London: Routledge & Kegan Paul.

Weidman, L. M. (1997, May). *They called a game: The language television sportscasters use to describe athletes in the men's and women's NCAA basketball championships.* Paper presented at the annual conference of the International Communication Association, Montreal, Canada.

Wulf, S. (1993, February 22). Time to weed out the rooters: To those many broadcasters who are above all cheerleaders, I say, 'Boooooo.' *Sports Illustrated, 78,* 190.

Subscription Order Form

Please ❑ enter ❑ renew my subscription to

RESEARCH ON LANGUAGE
AND SOCIAL INTERACTION
Volume 32, 1999, Quarterly

Subscription prices per volume:

Individual: ❑ $35.00 (US/Canada)   ❑ $65.00 (All Other Countries)

Institution: ❑ $225.00 (US/Canada)   ❑ $255.00 (All Other Countries)

Subscriptions are entered on a calendar-year basis only and must be prepaid in US currency -- check, money order, or credit card. **Offer expires 12/31/99. NOTE: Institutions must pay institutional rates.** Individual subscription orders paid by institutional checks will be returned.

❑ Payment Enclosed

Total Amount Enclosed $_____

❑ Charge My Credit Card

❑ VISA ❑ MasterCard ❑ AMEX ❑ Discover

Exp. Date_____

Card Number _____

Signature _____
(Credit card orders cannot be processed without your signature.)

Please print clearly to ensure proper delivery.

Name _____

Address _____

_____

City _____ State _____ Zip+4 _____
Prices are subject to change without notice.

Lawrence Erlbaum Associates, Inc.
Journal Subscription Department
10 Industrial Avenue, Mahwah, NJ 07430
(201) 236-9500   FAX (201) 236-0072

SOCIAL AND COGNITIVE APPROACHES TO INTERPERSONAL COMMUNICATION

Edited by
Susan R. Fussell
Carnegie Mellon University
Roger J. Kreuz
University of Memphis

"This solid contribution to research in the field will be appreciated not only by psycholinguistics, but more generally by cognitive and social psychologists as well."

--Choice

Historically, the social aspects of language use have been considered the domain of social psychology, while the underlying psycholinguistic mechanisms have been the purview of cognitive psychology. Recently, it has become increasingly clear that these two dimensions are highly interrelated: cognitive mechanisms underlying speech production and comprehension interact with social psychological factors, such as beliefs about one's interlocutors and politeness norms, and with the dynamics of the conversation itself, to produce shared meaning. This realization has led to an exciting body of research integrating the social and cognitive dimensions which has greatly increased our understanding of human language use.

Each chapter in this volume demonstrates how the theoretical approaches and research methods of social and cognitive psychology can be successfully interwoven to provide insight into one or more fundamental questions about the process of interpersonal communication. The topics under investigation include the nature and role of speaker intentions in the communicative process, the production and comprehension of indirect speech and figurative language, perspective-taking and conversational collaboration, and the relationships between language, cognition, culture, and social interaction. The book will be of interest to all those who study interpersonal language use: social and cognitive psychologists, theoretical and applied linguists, and communication researchers.

Contents: **Part I:** *Introduction and Background.* **S.R. Fussell, R.J. Kreuz,** Social and Cognitive Approaches to Interpersonal Communication: Introduction and Overview. **R.W. Gibbs, Jr.,** The Varieties of Intentions in Interpersonal Communication. **N. Schwarz,** Communication in Standardized Research Situations: A Gricean Perspective. **Part II:** *Indirect Speech Acts and Figurative Language.* **T. Holtgraves,** Interpersonal Foundations of Conversational Indirectness. **R.J. Kreuz, M.A. Kassler, L. Coppenrath,** The Use of Exaggeration in Discourse: Cognitive and Social Facets. **S.R. Fussell, M.M. Moss,** Figurative Language in Emotional Communication. **Part III:** *Perspective-Taking and Conversational Collaboration.* **M.F. Schober,** Different Kinds of Conversational Perspective-Taking. **B. Keysar,** Language Users as Problem Solvers: Just What Ambiguity Problem Do They Solve? **S.E. Brennan,** The Grounding Problem in Conversations With and Through Computers. **Part IV:** *Cognition, Language, and Social Interaction.* **G.R. Semin,** Cognition, Language, and Communication. **C-Y. Chiu, R.M. Krauss, I.Y-M. Lau,** Some Cognitive Consequences of Communication.

0-8058-2269-0 [cloth] / 1998 / 312pp. / $59.95
0-8058-2270-4 [paper] / 1998 / 312pp. / $32.50

Lawrence Erlbaum Associates, Inc.
10 Industrial Avenue, Mahwah, NJ 07430
201/236–9500   FAX 201/760–3735

Prices subject to
change without notice.

Call toll-free to order: 1-800-9-BOOKS-9...9am to 5pm EST only.
e-mail to: orders@erlbaum.com
visit LEA's web site at http://www.erlbaum.com

VALIDATION IN LANGUAGE ASSESSMENT

Edited by
Anthony J. Kunnan
California State University, Los Angeles

"This notable volume contributes significant, unique information to researchers, educators, and graduate students whose work focuses on language testing. Each chapter presents a validation study in depth, describing a particular approach to validation research, a unique set of findings, and useful implications for future inquiry and practice in language testing. As a whole, the volume helps to advance knowledge in this area and displays a range of important, innovative orientations to research."

--Alistair Cumming
Ontario Institute for Studies in Education

Validation in Language Assessment contributes to the variety of validation approaches and analytical and interpretive techniques only recently adopted by language assessment researchers. Featuring selected papers from the 17th Language Testing Research Colloquium, the volume presents diverse approaches with an international perspective on validation in language assessment.

0-8058-2752-8 [cloth] / 1998 / 304pp. / $59.95
0-8058-2753-6 [paper] / 1998 / 304pp. / $32.50

Lawrence Erlbaum Associates, Inc.
10 Industrial Avenue, Mahwah, NJ 07430
201/236-9500   FAX 201/236-0072

Prices subject to change without notice.

Call toll-free to order: 1-800-9-BOOKS-9...9am to 5pm EST only.
e-mail to: orders@erlbaum.com
visit LEA's web site at http://www.erlbaum.com

FACE[T]S OF FIRST LANGUAGE LOSS

Sandra G. Kouritzin
University of British Columbia

This book contributes to the understanding of first-language loss in both immigrant and indigenous communities in (at least) three ways. First, it provides insight into the process of language loss and the factors contributing to it. Second, it attempts to define, from an insider perspective, what it means to "lose" a language. Third, it analyzes the perceived consequences of first language loss in terms of social, academic, emotional, and economic factors -- an approach previously lacking in research on language loss.

Most studies of first language loss are impersonal, even when they tell emotional stories. This polyphonic book about language loss and imperfect learning of heritage languages tells the inside story. Easy to read and yet academic, it gives voice to five different storytellers who relate the histories of their first language loss and analyzes themes from 21 life-history case studies of adults who had lost their first languages while learning English. The stories in this book make a compelling argument that heritage languages should be preserved, that ESL should be about developing bilinguals not English monolinguals.

Important reading for researchers, practitioners, and graduate students in ESL and bilingual education, multicultural education, cultural studies, and sociology, this book will also interest qualitative researchers as an example of a unique form of both doing and writing research.

Contents: Preface. Introduction. On What Pretext?: A Pre/text for Language Loss Research. **Part I:** *Face-Touching: A Story-Book.* A Musical Interlude: Ariana: Introduction. Ariana's Story: But I'm Canadian-Born. Richard: Introduction. Richard's Story: English Is a Full-Time Job. Lara: Introduction. Lara's Story: An Outsider Looking In. Brian: Introduction. Brian's Story: Nothing Too Deep. Helena: Introduction. Helena's Story: Learning the Rules. **Part II:** *Dwelling in the Borderlands.* Borders: Introduction. Family Relationships. Self-Image and Cultural Identity. School Relationships. School Performance. The Meaning of Loss. Discordance: Conclusion: Not a Finale: A Decrescendo. **Appendices:** Life History Selection Criteria. Subject Biographical Information.
0-8058-3185-1 [cloth] / 1999 / 248pp. / $49.95
0-8058-3186-X [paper] / 1999 / 248pp. / $22.50

Lawrence Erlbaum Associates, Inc.

10 Industrial Avenue, Mahwah, NJ 07430
201/236–9500   FAX 201/760–3735

Prices subject to
change without notice.

Call toll-free to order: 1-800-9-BOOKS-9...9am to 5pm EST only.
e-mail to: orders@erlbaum.com
visit LEA's web site at http://www.erlbaum.com